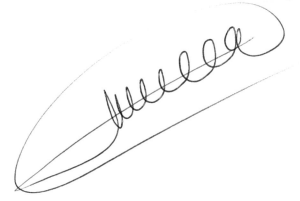

What Real Estate Gurus Don't Tell You

Why Some Succeed While Others Struggle

By Marc Mousseau

1-888-397-6272
1-888-397-MARC

marc@mmousseau.com
www.whatrealestategurusdonttellyou.com
www.WREGDTY.com
www.mmousseau.com

Copyright @2013 Marc Mousseau
All rights reserved.

No part of this book may be reproduced or transmitted in any forms or by any means, electronic or mechanical, including photocopying, recording, or by any information storage and retrieval system, without permission, in writing from the author.

ISBN-13:
978-1493643219

ISBN-10:
1493643215

WHAT REAL ESTATE GURUS DON'T TELL YOU

Foreword

There are two kinds of speakers, trainers and coaches in this world. We have the ones that had become famous thanks to the books they have published, their TV appearances and/or radio interviews, and then we have the ones that you'll never ever hear or know about, the 'stealth' trainers and coaches.

The stealth speakers, trainers and coaches might steal the show. Fortunately, through this book you will have a chance to meet one. Marc Mousseau is going to inspire you and teach you what he is doing himself - things he has learned through the wisdom that comes from "hard knocks". He has applied what he teaches into his own life and business in order to become one of the best coaches and trainers that I have ever come across.

For 30 years, Marc has been coached by some of the best: Tony Robbins, Jay Abraham and many others. He invested time and constant effort in himself to become one of the best North American Real Estate trainers out there and that the reason why he coaches some of my best clients. I give him the responsibility to coach my preferred clients, because I have unconditional trust in him and his professional knowledge.

When Marc came to me with this book idea that he had, I challenged him to write it under my 10–10–10 author program, and he did. The book is brilliant! It introduces the transformational knowledge that you need to have in order to succeed in Real Estate and explains why so many people fail to become Real Estate Entrepreneurs.

Marc has spoken with me at my World Connect event in September of this year. He has dazzled our audience with his speaking style, his conviction, his knowledge, his passion and "the don't tell me I can't do it" attitude that he has! I will welcome Marc to any of my stages anytime, because he is now one to follow - one that you will hear about!

So, it is with pleasure that I want to introduce:

"What Real Estate Gurus Don't Tell You"
Why Some Succeed While Others Struggle

~ Raymond Aaron, New York Times Best Selling Author

Acknowledgements

I would like to acknowledge a very important person to me that had a major impact in my life a few months ago. His name is Raymond Aaron. **www.aaron.com**

For the past two and a half years I've been working on writing a book called *"What Real Estate Gurus Don't Tell You" or you would have to pay a fortune to get!* and never got to finish it.

Eight weeks ago, on October 25th, 2013, Raymond challenged me to write a completely new book for this series and the challenge was to do it in less then 10 weeks.

This book is part of the series *"What Real Estate Gurus Don't Tell You"* and I believe that this book is a great preamble, a great foundation explaining why some succeed and what you need to do and know about getting into real estate.

I made that commitment!

I want to thank Raymond for encouraging me and giving me that little extra push to write and produce this book in less than 10 weeks. His 10–10–10 program detailed exactly what I had to do. He is a great coach and the perfect example showing that if you follow what your coach tells you to do, you will succeed!

My book may not be regarded as a literary marvel, but it comes from my genuine real estate experience and background. Again, thank you Raymond for challenging me to write this book under your 10–10–10 program.

I also want to thank my graphic designer David Beaud (www.davidbeaud.com) for doing great work on my personal website and designing these book covers. Thanks also to my editor Pavel Terziev for putting this book together and for doing what I can't do!

Dedication

I dedicate this book to my wife Lori, for believing in me and trusting me to write this book. I have been talking about writing a book for more than 10 years and now it's done. I thank her not only for supporting me, but also for believing that I had something valuable to teach other people to get them free both financially and from oppression. You are the love of my life!

I want to thank my two children Alexandre (25) and Marika (22) for being such great children. They will both always be my children regardless of their age. They liberate my life and make me so proud! They are growing to be wonderful adults. Love you both!

I want to thank my mom, for having instilled in me the values that I have and what I give to people surrounding me. You cannot take that away!

One who I can't forget is my brother Louis. He has always been in my shadow, but with a heart to give to others that no one can match. He has been a life supporter of all my endeavors and I thank him for being there.

To my mother and father-in-law, thank you for being so wonderful and supporting both Lori and me in our lives.

As I am writing this dedication **today, November 18th, 2013,** *I make a special dedication to my father that passed away, two years ago to this day.*

Dad, you have always been proud of me and today as I complete this dedication, and write these final words, I just want to say that without you I would not be the man that I am!

Thank You!

Marc

Who Am I?

Marc Mousseau
Business Strategist and Real Estate Catalyst.

You hear it all the time from a myriad of entrepreneurs with different backgrounds, long before they were running successful businesses, their entrepreneurial spirit was alive. While some kids were selling lemonade on the street corner or inventing gadgets in the basement, Marc, at the tender age of three, saw his first business opportunity and just couldn't resist taking advantage of it.

Marc naively believed that the crate of empty milk bottles the milkman left on the corner of his parent's lot each week was going to be thrown out. Knowing that the local store owner would happily give him five cents for each bottle, Marc decided not to let those bottles go to waste. Each week he would take two bottles to the store and trade them in for easy money to "invest" in candy - good idea? Of course, until his father found out!

Although his fledgling business plans may have been halted rather abruptly, the entrepreneurial spirit of the young boy had already taken root. By the time Marc turned nineteen, his heart and vision encouraged him to drop out of school to pursue his business interests.

While his dad was more than upset by Marc's decision to abandon school, a few short years later he simply couldn't deny his son's entrepreneurial success.

At twenty-two years old, the inexperienced, and "undereducated" Marc had already created a very profitable car detailing business and was making more money than his father.

Marc's mindset for seizing opportunities that others couldn't see had already begun to emerge. Since then, Marc has built many successful and profitable businesses - a small start-up car detailing company, a flight school, a multi-million dollar real estate project in Central America and even in the wine business!

By the time he turned twenty-four, Marc had decided to buy his first house - a townhouse in a brand new development. Then, shortly before Marc was to move in, the developer went bankrupt, leaving the fifty-two-unit project (and Marc's house) unfinished. Guess what? Marc's deposit money would have been lost if he hadn't taken action - and he did.

With absolutely no Real Estate experience under his belt up until that moment, Marc simply couldn't afford the luxury to be scared or perplexed by the situation. He was bold enough to approach the bankruptcy trustee, and he succeeded in acquiring the rights to the entire project.

After two years of hard work, he assigned his rights to another developer for $250,000, who finished the houses and decided to keep Marc on as General Manager of Operations and Sales - in order to be able to use his energy, valuable skills, and talents.

With the success of this first deal under his belt, Marc couldn't defy his entrepreneurial instincts, nor stay blind to the incredible and infinite potential of the Real Estate business. He had already realized the power of Real Estate to generate income.

Meanwhile, a local Real Estate development company had taken notice of Marc's success and asked him to join their team. For the next ten years, Marc was invited to take on the role of a Junior Partner in the company, working on many Real Estate deals, managing financing, steering the marketing of the projects, acquisition, and being responsible for handling investor relations for more than 1,500 condominium units.

By 1994, Marc was eager, but feeling ready to venture out on his own, and decided to open his own property management company. That's how Westmark Development Inc. came to be. Operating out of Edmonton, Alberta, soon Marc's company was responsible for the management of more than 1,100 units. He became a real estate broker and sold more then 600 units in 3 years.

Through it all, he has experienced the successes, celebrations, and at times failures—common to every business owner - but Marc has always found the right way to overcome the hard challenges and contribute to the sustainable growth of his companies and business projects.

It wasn't until a few years later that Marc's life purpose was realized. Approached by two of the leading United States-based Real Estate training companies, Whitney Education Group and Tigrent Learning, to help start their Canadian operations, Marc was asked to both develop the course curriculum *and* become a trainer himself. After a few years Robert Kiyosaky (*Rich Dad, Poor Dad*) acquired the company and Marc became one of their top trainers!

Since then, Marc has delivered high-energy, information-packed training sessions to students on a range of Real Estate topics including topics like foreclosure, lease options, land development, wholesale, property management, buy-rent-hold strategies, syndication, condo conversion and by-laws, contracts, negotiation, and creative finance. His training and mentoring have inspired and motivated thousands of students to become successful Real Estate investors and joyfully live their ultimate life.

Internationally recognized speaker, trainer and author, having lectured on 3 continents - North America, the United States and South Africa, Marc has revealed to over 35,000 real estate investors and business owners the secrets of the most vital aspects of real estate, namely how to break through mindset barriers and constantly think out of the box, and how to easily achieve new levels of success in their undertakings.

Today his entrepreneurial spirit hasn't abandoned him and he continues to invest in Real Estate in Canada and the United States, boldly taking on the big contemporary challenge of focusing on distressed areas hardest hit by the credit crisis.

With over 37 years of in-the-trenches entrepreneurial experience, Marc truly understands the fears and challenges faced by everyday real estate investors and business owners, from those just getting started to seasoned professionals.

His transformational and adaptive coaching style, and **"don't tell me I can't"** attitude inspires investors and entrepreneurs to show the courage and the will needed to break through barriers and accelerate their path to financial success.

Today, Marc's passion for training and interacting with the next generation of real estate businessmen and women remains strong.

Often questioned by students about why he teaches when he could make more money putting Real Estate deals together, Marc simply refers to his deep and honest inner belief, that educating and sharing his experience is his true life purpose.

"To Grow,
To Educate Others
And To Release Them To Freedom!"

After all, what is more energizing than giving people the courage and the knowledge to live their dreams?!

For more information, please contact Marc at:

- 1-888-397- MARC (6242)
- marc@mmousseau.com

Visit our websites at:

- www.WhatRealEstateGurusDontTellYou.com
- www.WREGDTY.com
- www.mmousseau.com

Testimonials

Here is a list of testimonials that I have accumulated over a period of time, while training.

"Over-delivers Rich Content In An Informative And Entertaining Way!"

Marc led my first Real Estate Investment course back in 2009 with Rich Dad Education. I was extremely satisfied with Marc's presentation, as he over-delivered rich content in an informative and entertaining way. It was a pleasure to participate. As a result of training with Marc for an entire weekend, I got tools, built the foundation and began the path of working on myself (instead of on my job), with my heart fully committed to the game! Four years later, I no longer have to "work" for my income that covers my living expenses. I now have the freedom to live life on my terms...and this is just the beginning! Merci Marc! C'est Bon!

~ Dominik Kawa, February 14th, 2013

"Marc Delivers Content Rich Information!"

The first time I heard Marc speak at a Real Estate weekend event, he emphasized how a little bit of information can be dangerous. I was planning to invest into Real Estate, and knew I needed to get better educated. We have taken several Real Estate trainings from Marc and benefited greatly from his experience and teachings. It helped us with smart negotiating with vendors, drawing up contracts and designing clauses, and structuring our assets for protection. Marc Mousseau delivers information-rich and interesting courses that held our attention throughout. He's a great presenter and teacher. If anyone is planning to invest in Real Estate, they should learn from Marc to get educated first to avoid costly mistakes. Our investment into training has paid us back many times over.

~ Jan & Rey Laferriere, March 3rd, 2013

"Thanks To Marc, 74K in Profit On My First Deal!"

I was thinking about buying a six-unit industrial building and it was a good thing I spent some money learning how to do it, Thanks to Marc and the education I took I figured out how to do it RIGHT! By the way, I sold it last year in September for a 74K profit. Not bad for me, as I only make $14.50 per hour at my job!

~ Posted by Pam on February 2nd, 2010

"Mousseau Is an Excellent Teacher! I Am On My Way To Financial Freedom At the Age Twenty-three."

If you want out of the rat race, you need to educate yourself to achieve it, duh! My wife and I have trained under Marc Mousseau's guidance and his fellow colleagues. What we learned enabled us to purchase and create some major lake development projects. Mousseau is an excellent teacher. He knows Real Estate investing inside-out and has acquired his knowledge through real experience. Thank you for sharing your knowledge Marc!

~ Stefan Aarnio, May 2012

"I Wish We Knew That 5 Years Ago!"

By the time my brother and I took the training, we kept looking at each other saying, "Man, I wished we knew that five years ago!" We're not investors at all. Real investors know how to work the numbers. They can make real deals happen. Learning how to creatively finance projects is something we learned from Marc and how to treat this as a business as well.

~ *Marco Silvestri*

"The Light Bulbs Just Kept Going Off!"

When I met Marc at his first training, the light bulbs just kept going off. I kept thinking, "Really? You can do that?" or "I didn't know you could do that." I said to myself, "If I had known this before I bought what I bought, I would have been way better off and would not have made these mistakes. This got me to take even more training: Creative Financing, Land Development, Condo Conversion. Marc had a big influence on what I wanted to do, what I wanted to learn, and what I aspired to be.

~ *Ken Chung, December, 2012*

"Mark Blew The Door Off Its Hinges And Allowed Me To Have A Job That Isn't Really A Job"

When I began my investing career the door was open a crack, but Mark blew the door off its hinges. His insight into the world of making money through various Real Estate strategies has created opportunities that I would not [have] considered before his training. It has also led to other non-real estate opportunities. What started as a way to supplement my income has turned out to be career that has not only significantly improved my net worth, but has allowed me to have a job that isn't really a job. Time with Mark is time well spent.

~ *Jeff Harada, Real Estate Investments and Consulting, September 26th, 2012*

"Provides Years Of Knowledge!"

Marc is a very driven, enthusiastic Real Estate mentor/instructor. He has provided years of knowledge to his students who, in turn, became my clients. I have witnessed that his techniques has proven to be one of the key components in their success.

~ *Carmen Campagnaro, President of Pro Funds Mortgages, December 31st, 2010*

"A True Visionary! Always on the Look Out for a Win Win!"

Marc Mousseau is a true visionary in the Real Estate industry. Marc endeavors to find win-win solutions for all parties involved in every transaction he enters. Marc has taught students from around the world how to transform their lives through Real Estate.

~ Darren Plumb, January 13th, 2013

"Today It Feels Like A Breakthrough I've Been In Need Of!"

Thanks for a great coaching session today. As you know, there's been a lot of flux in my work situation and this has hampered my ability to make a decision and move forward with it. And in fact, another two things have happened in the last few days that have brought further confusion to the general state of affairs. I have been grappling with trying to create clarity in the midst of a murky situation. Today's session felt like the muddy waters becoming clearer. It feels like the breakthrough I've been in need of. I look forward to continuing to gain clarity, perspective and the guidance to progress. Thank you!

~ Dr. Kay Mathabe, Urologist

"Another Satisfied Student"

I took Marc Mousseau's Investing Bootcamp this weekend! Before taking the Bootcamp, I thought I was a pretty savvy investor, but the things I learned from Marc just blew me away. I now realize what I had learned and what I was currently learning was not nearly enough to make the difference between investing in residential real estate to becoming a potential commercial investor. If you are thinking of transforming yourself from a real estate investor into a real estate entrepreneur, then you must take Marc's course! I can only imagine where I will be a year from now!

~ A. Mohamed, December, 2013

Table Of Contents

FOREWORD 4

ACKNOWLEDGEMENTS 6

DEDICATION 8

WHO AM I? 10

TESTIMONIALS 16

CHAPTER I: *Why Do Some Real Estate Investors Succeed While Others Struggle?* 25
    1.1 - Are You a Real Estate Investor Or a Real Estate Entrepreneur? 30

CHAPTER II: *10 Key Components To Success* 33
    2.1 - #1 Ratio Of Success 34
    2.2 - #2 Coach And Mentor 37
    2.3 - #3 Partnership 40
        2.3.1 - Spouse Or Life Partner 40
        2.3.2 - Business Partner 41
        2.3.3 - The Partner That You Blame Everything On 42
    2.4 - #4 Limiting Beliefs 44
    2.5 - #5 Self-discipline 46
    2.6 - #6 Go Big Or Go Home 50
    2.7 - #7 Realtor 51
    2.8 - #8 Knowing Your Strengths 52
    2.9 - #9 Patience 54
    2.10 - #10 Commitments 55

CHAPTER III: Do You Have a Plan? 57
        3.1 - How Many Offers Do You Need In Order
               To Achieve Your Goal? 61

CHAPTER IV: What Kind Of Property Should You Buy? 67
        4.1 - Single Family Homes 67
        4.2 - Multi-Units and Multi-Unit Walk-ups 70
        4.3 - Multi High-Rise 71
        4.4 - Multi High-Rise With Amenities 72
        4.5 - Commercial Real Estate 72
        4.6 – Land 73

CHAPTER V: Are You Branded? Who Are You? 75
        5.1 - Personal Branding 76
        5.2 - Who Are You? 76
        5.3 - Phone Line 81
        5.4 - Business Cards 82
        5.5 - Are You a "yahoo"? 85
        5.6 - How To Talk To Millionaires? 85

CHAPTER VI: Making Offers On Property - Buying Techniques .. 88
        6.1 - Shotgun Approach 89
        6.2 - Low Ball Approach 89
        6.3 - Pre-Framing 90
        6.4 - The Dating Principle Approach 92
        6.5 - Negotiations 95
        6.6 - Maximum Allowable Purchase Price
              Or "MAPP" 97

CHAPTER VII: Looking For a No Money Down Deal 99
        7.1 Do No Money Down Deals Really Exist? 100
        7.2 Should You Only Look For
              No Money Down Deals? 101

CHAPTER VIII: How To Find a Deal? 105

8.1 - The Vendor Must Like You 106
8.2 - Think Creatively Right From The Get-Go! 106
8.3 - Find a Motivated Vendor! 106
8.4 - Looking For Distressed Properties 109
8.5 - Is There Equity On This Property Or Not? 109
8.6 - Do You Really Need This Property
       In Your Portfolio? 110

CHAPTER IX: Key Priorities To Buying a Real Estate 113
9.1 - Priority #1: You Make Money
       When You Buy Real Estate 113
9.2 - Priority #2: You Will Profit When You Sell 114
9.3 - Priority #3: Does This Property Cash-Flow?
       Yes or No? 114
9.4 - Priority #4: Cash-on-Cash Return 116
9.5 - Priority #5: Having Good Terms
       and Conditions 117
9.6 - Priority #6: State Of Repairs 117
9.7 - Priority #7: Is The Area Where I Am
       Purchasing The Property Appreciating? 117

CHAPTER X: The Art Of Negotiations 119
10.1 - Will My First Offer Be The Final One? 119
10.2 - Working With Multiple Offers 121
10.3 - Being Prepared Is Key To Successful
        Negotiations 122
10.4 - Should I View The Property
        Before Making an Offer 124

CHAPTER XI: Do You Have Any Money? 127
11.1 - Should You Train
        Your Real Estate Agent? 128
11.2 - How To Ask For Money? 131
11.3 - Should You Go To Your Bank? 132
11.4 - Where Will You Find Money? 133

11.5 - How Much Money Should You Pay Your Financial Partners? 134

CHAPTER XII: Six Stumbling Blocks That Will Prevent You From Succeeding And 4 Tips That Will Get You Started! 135

12.1 - #1 Stumbling Block: Who Do You Hang Around With? 135
12.2 - #2 Stumbling Block: Watch Who You Take Advice From! 136
13.3 - #3 Stumbling Block: Biggest Time-Wasters 137
13.4 - #4 Stumbling Block: People's Addiction To Computer Games 139
13.5 - #5 Stumbling Block: Attending Free Seminars . 140
13.6 - #6 Stumbling Block: TV Shows Promoting House-Flipping 141
13.7 - Tip #1: Learn . . . Learn . . . Learn! 142
13.8 - Tip #2: Learn From Other People's Mistakes, Not Yours! 143
13.9 - Tip #3: Implementation Is Key To Success! 143
13.10 - Tip #4: Get Coached And Be Accountable! 143

CHAPTER XIII: Where Do I Go From Here? 145

13.1 - Look Where Other People Aren't 147
13.2 - Buying From Developers 149
13.3 - Quick Math 150
13.4 - Quick Tip 151

CHAPTER XIV: What Is Your Exit Strategy? 153

14.1 - Buyer Beware 155

CHAPTER XV: The 29 Second Pitch 157

15.1 - Who Are You? 157

CONCLUSION 160

BONUSES 161

BOOKS FROM THE AUTHOR 163

Chapter I

Why Do Some Real Estate Investors Succeed While Others Struggle

A few months ago while talking with my wife about real estate success, we began to question why some investors are successful, while others simply flounder. Throughout my career, I've always questioned myself about that conundrum and I believe I have finally found the reason. It's quite simple actually.

As you read in my introduction, I have 30 years of experience in real estate and business. I have taught close to 35,000 new and seasoned real estate investors over the last 15 years on how to succeed in this dynamic business.

I know many of my students personally and some of them have become very very successful - some have even become millionaires. Most of them went from unemployed to full-time real estate investors. Some of them actually made the decision to quit their jobs and become full-time real estate entrepreneurs. What is it about these people that made them so successful? What did they do differently that others did not?

I decided to find out, so I picked up the phone and started calling all my former students that I knew had succeeded. I was looking for a common denominator explaining their success. And I found it!

I basically taught the same thing to all of my 35,000 students. They had all received the same **"transactional"** knowledge and yet, some of them made it big and others did not. I toured some potential investment properties and ran through the financial analysis with them, from top to bottom and from bottom to top. I began to study the path that my successful students had taken. I looked for other key components that contributed to their success.

What I discovered was one essential commonality. They had all mastered what I call the **"transformational"** aspects of real estate and entrepreneurship.

For me, "transformational" is what real estate gurus won't ever tell you. It's a systematic process of learning who you need to be, what you need to do and what you need to avoid doing in order for you to become a successful real estate investor, and to take it one step further, a real estate entrepreneur. And the truth is the big gurus simply don't teach the "transformational" in all those expensive seminars.

The reason why one person succeeds versus the other is not only the **transactional** knowledge that these investors had acquired. It was in fact, their **transformational** knowledge that made them successful.

The **transformational** side is what the real estate gurus aren't telling you and is exactly what I will be talking about in this book. These are the well-hidden secrets of this business. It is the "secret sauce" that my successful students applied to the **transactional** knowledge I taught them in my courses.

In this book I'll be giving the answers to some of the most vital questions, like:
- What is it that you need to do?
- Who do you need to become?
- How do you keep from being discouraged?
- How do you brand yourself?
- How do you make a strategic plan?
- How can you have a negotiating mindset?
- How do you deal with the scarcity of money?
- How do you avoid stumbling blocks?
- Where do you start?
- What should you buy?
- Should you start little or go big?
- What are the "no money down" hurdles?
- Where do you need to look for properties?
- Which seminar should you go to?
- What is your belief system?
- What impact does it have on you?

First and foremost, all of this will transform you as a person. We need to transform you as a person in order for you to put into action what I teach as **transactional** and to apply it.

So **transformational**, in other words, is really about transforming your mindset, your thoughts, your ideas, your views, your brand, your image, your purpose, your mission and your life knowledge in general. Only then we can apply the theory of real estate.

It's critical to understand that only by mastering both the **transformational** and the **transactional**, you would be able to become a successful real estate entrepreneur.

The first thing I need to do is to change your mindset. **I really need you to start thinking outside of the box.** I need you to look at yourself differently than yesterday, so that you can give yourself a chance to become that successful person - **THE ENTREPRENEUR**.

If you were to do a search on Google for a list of entrepreneurial characteristics, I'm sure you'd find many common denominators, or traits, that many successful entrepreneurs have in common, regardless of the business sector they are operating in. But let me share with you what I think the "magical" characteristics are that make these wealthy entrepreneurs unique:

- They always do what they enjoy.
- They take their business seriously.
- They plan everything thoroughly.

- They manage their money wisely.
- They are not afraid to ask for the sale.
- They have the courage to ask for commitment.
- They know that it's all about their customers.
- They become shameless self-promoters. They are absolutely aware of the fact that it's vital for all real estate investors to be able to promote themselves in order to thrive. Often this happens through their website, through their business cards and through their image or dress code.
- They have mastered the ability to project a positive and successful business image.
- They know how to use technology to assist them.
- They get to know their customer - who they are; what they are looking for; what they want to buy.
- They have a great business team.
- They become known experts in their field.
- They know exactly how to create a competitive advantage.
- They are accessible.
- They are active and involved - not only in their business ventures, but in the community as well.
- They have mastered the art of negotiation.
- They have designed their work space and work flow with purpose - where they work; how they work; what they do.
- They are organized.

- They remain focused on their goals, they don't jump at every opportunity or try to do everything.
- They know that taking time off is essential for mental and physical health and is also a great time for brainstorming. And they know exactly when to do it.
- And maybe the most important aspect - they follow up, follow up, follow up!

These are the critical traits of a successful business person. Take a moment to go back through the list and have an honest conversation with yourself. *Which of these characteristics do you already possess? Which ones might you need to work on developing?*

As you read through this book, I want you to consciously look at your mindset. What thoughts and beliefs do you currently have about your ability to have success as a real estate entrepreneur? My goal is to give you the tools you need to start changing your mindset and to develop the characteristics that will set you on the path to success and wealth.

Are You a Real Estate <u>Investor</u> Or a Real Estate <u>Entrepreneur</u>?

For me, the definition of a real estate investor is somebody who has bought at least his or her own personal property. The day you buy a house guess what happens? You have instantly become a real estate investor!

When someone buys their first property, they usually put a deposit down - let's say it's 25%. Then they borrow the balance of 75% from a bank. What they are actually doing is investing into an asset. Essentially, they are investing a bit of money every month for 25 years (amortization time), until the property is paid for and they own it. They hope it will be worth more than what they paid for it originally. Therefore, it is an investment!

Remember that you don't actually own the property (asset) until it is paid for. **The reality is that the bank owns it.** So, when you buy your first property, you become a real estate investor. But that is not enough!

In order for you to succeed in real estate and to make money out of it, you need to become an entrepreneur. You absolutely need to make it a business. You cannot just dibble-dabble in it whenever you feel like it.

YOU ABSOLUTELY HAVE TO COMMIT!

If you don't truly commit, the moment something goes wrong, and it happens to every investor at some point, you will simply quit and say, "I knew this wouldn't work out!".

So first and foremost, I want you to become **a real estate entrepreneur**. This is a life changing decision and one that I am hoping you are willing to make. Real estate entrepreneurs know the value of being entrepreneurs. They know what advantages it will give them, their family, their grandchildren and the legacy that they'll leave.

What I want for you is to become a real estate entrepreneur, not just a real estate investor. I am going to give you the tools in this book to become just that!

Chapter II
10 Key Components to Success

What does it really take for a person to succeed in real estate investing? This chapter is meant to establish a strong knowledge base for you. There are specific key criteria, key ideas and concepts that you absolutely must understand in order to thrive in this business.

First, I'm going to give you an outline of each component, then we will go deeper into each one of them.

In order for you to succeed in the competitive and challenging environment of real estate, you must know the following:

These are the key ingredients that will allow you to succeed in the real estate business.

#1 Ratio Of Success — *What should you expect as your closing ratio when you're presenting offers to purchase property?* Knowing the ratio of success will make sure that you don't get discouraged for no reason.

One of the biggest challenges with new investors I have noticed throughout my career, is that they usually expect to look at 6-7 different properties, to make 2-3 offers of purchase, and expect to close on at least one of those deals! They simply hope that one of these properties will be a good deal and generate cash flow.

The reality though has nothing to do with this assumption. Remember that this is a numbers game. There are thousands and thousands of properties out there available for sale and **your main priority should always be to look for the best deal on the market, no matter what**. Always keep that in mind!

As a real estate entrepreneur, you understand that you need to make offers in order for you to find a good deal. It doesn't matter if you have to make 9, 57, or 99 offers on properties. You need to find the right one for you.

If you understand the following ratio and you're willing to put the necessary work into it, you will succeed.

The ratio of success is very simple, it is 50–6–2–1. *What does that mean?* You'll need to make 50 offers, 6 of them will be accepted, 2 will be acceptable to you, and you will close on 1!

Why would there be only 6 accepted of the 50 offers that you put out? Because you make offers on property based on your buying criteria, not what the vendor wants.

You don't care about what the vendor wants for the property, you know what you should pay for the property! **It has to be a good deal. The numbers have to make sense!**

So now, you have 6 accepted deals - *why would only 2 of them be acceptable?* Because you will find things that don't add up while you are doing your due diligence. Some things won't work for you. You might not be able to get financing, or you won't find a partner etc., therefore you will pull out of a few deals.

So, you have 2 properties that are acceptable. Now ask yourself the following questions:
1) Is this the best investment for me **NOW**, at this particular moment?
2) What is my exit strategy?
3) In the worst case scenario, which property would I **want** to keep, and which can I **afford** to keep?

Now if the answer to the first question is "yes", if you know what your **exit strategy** should be and you answer "yes" to question #3, then you should buy it. But in case you still have some doubts, you should only pick one of them.

Now, I am sure some of you think: "I want to buy with no money down".

If this is your only criteria for buying, then your ratio of success becomes 100–6–2–1. This means that you'll have to make 100 offers, 6 will be accepted, 2 will be acceptable, and you will close on 1 of these with no money down. You should not get discouraged. You can still purchase this way.

When I start a new training session, one of the first things I tell my students is to go to a Office Depot, Staples, etc., and buy a filing cabinet and 100 file folders. You should do the same thing.

Then I want you to number the folders 1–100. Knowing that the ratio will pay off and that this is a numbers game, your job is to fill each one of them with an offer.

Bear in mind that you will need to make at least 50 offers to find a good deal. And 100, if you want a 'no money down' deal.

Don't forget - the ratio of success is 50–6–2–1. For a 'no money down' deal it is 100-6-2-1. That will help you stay focused!

This is where most new real estate investors fail, because they don't have the necessary patience. They want the first few properties that they look at to be a good deal and or a "no money down" deal instead of using the ratio formula.

#2 Coach And Mentor — *What is the difference between having a coach and a mentor? Why would you want a coach?*

Do you have a coach or a mentor? Some of you say, "I do have a mentor. My mentor is a friend of mine, he's my dad's uncle and he'll help me. He'll mentor me in the right way".

This is all good, but there is a significant difference between a coach and a mentor. The biggest one is that **you are not accountable to a mentor and you are to a coach**.

Your coach is there to give you advice based on his experience. He is there to hold your hand when you feel scared, he is there to make sure that you follow trough on your goals. He is there to take you out of your comfort zone. He is there to put a plan together, to implement it with you, to measure your success, to re-align it. He is there to make sure that you stick to your commitments, because his job is to make sure that you are accountable to him.

The coach is the professional who is responsible to give you specific instructions, like:
- ✓ Go buy a filing cabinet;
- ✓ Go buy a hundred file folders;
- ✓ Go buy a map;
- ✓ Go buy a set of darts;
- ✓ Go buy a domain name;
- ✓ Go get your first website up etc.;
- ✓ Call 15 agents next week;

- ✓ Prepare 3 offers;
- ✓ Get this information;
- ✓ Call this person;
- ✓ Review your documents.

IF YOU WANT TO LISTEN TO ONE
OF MY COACHING SESSIONS
WHERE I COACH ONE OF MY STUDENTS ON MAKING OFFERS ON A FEW PROPERTIES,
DOWNLOAD GREAT BONUSES AT:

www.mmousseau.com/bookbonuses

LISTEN CAREFULLY AND YOU WILL SEE WHAT COACHING IS ALL ABOUT! YOU WILL LEARN!

The coach will set timelines with you and require you to commit to them. He will expect these actions to be done by the time you have committed to have them done. The coach will remind you of your deadlines and will insist on you meeting them.

When you have your follow-up call with your coach and he asks, "Have you done what we had discussed and planned for?" and your response is "not really", his job is to give you a reality check.

It is not okay to break your commitments! Why would you pay him to coach you, if you are not willing to follow your plan? Don't forget that **this is not his plan, it is yours**!

You've made a commitment to succeed, you've made a commitment to do what's absolutely necessary, and if you're in breach of your commitment, the coach is the person that will hold you accountable for it.

By the way, a coach is a person that gets paid for his work. **HIS JOB IS TO COACH YOU!**

You may ask yourself, "What kind of coach should I get?" It's important to have a coach that has gone through the same process that you're currently going through, an experienced professional that knows what needs to be done in order for you to grow and succeed. The coach is there to help eliminate risk factors for you. A coach will save you a ton of money, because normally they have the experience you lack. He'll guide you the right way. That coach knows things and details that you are not aware of!

However, the coach should not be considered your friend. He is the guy that you have hired to show you the right things to do and the guy that you are accountable to.

I have coached hundreds of students, and if after two or three appointments they don't do what I expect out of them, and what we've committed to do, I tell them plain and simple that **they're wasting my time and their money.**

So, when it comes to making the decision - Coach or Mentor - get a coach! And don't tell me that your uncle, your real estate agent, or your dad's friend is your coach, because you are not accountable to them!

#3 Partnership

There are 3 different types of partnership:
1) Your spouse or your life partner.
2) Your real business partner.
3) The one that you blame everything on.

Spouse Or Life Partner

For those of you that are in this category and you want to get into real estate, the first concern that you have to address is the following: **you must make sure that your partner is in agreement with your plan.**

You have to realize that this is a joint venture business partnership that you're getting into. This is a business that both of you will benefit from and both of you must commit to. You should expect:
- to make sacrifices;
- time spent away making offers;
- time spent away looking at properties;

- having to make time to go to meetings;
- having to make time for training etc.

There has to be an education budget that both of you agree to, no matter what. You must be prepared for the necessary expenditure: money for training, money for attending meetings, money for traveling expenses etc.

Both of you have to keep each other from falling in love with a property. This is crucial! If both of you admit that you love the property, guess what? Price goes up and leverage goes down!

Business Partner

Should I have a partner? If you don't need one, don't get one, but often a partner will complement your strengths and will help with your weaknesses.

I really can't say that you should or should not have a business partner. Some people do great with partners, other without partners. Me and my student, friend and business partner Jean Lebeau were involved in a partnership in the Costa Rica project - the best partners that could be, the perfect complement.

My strengths were his weaknesses and my weaknesses his strengths. To give you an idea of this, we worked different hours - he liked to work nights, and I liked to work early, therefore as a partnership, we were working 20 hours a day.

The Partner That You Blame Everything On

I want you to have a business partner regardless if he is real or not!

You should always start a business conversation with: "My partner and I..."

Let me ask you this question - if you were to look at yourself in the mirror in the morning and say: "Partner, should we make an offer of purchase for this building today?", and if your partner answers "yes", as your business partner, he's given you specific instructions what to do, yes or no?

So, make the offer based on your partner's instruction. If he said no to that question, then you should tell the vendor or real estate agent that your partner said that we should pass on this opportunity, you get the drift here?

By the way guys, this is just a joke!

By having a partner you could:
- ✓ Put the blame for any hard decisions you make on someone else;
- ✓ Request different financial information;
- ✓ Negotiate harder;

- ✓ Say that your partner does not want the property anymore and that you want to buy it, but you can't under those circumstances etc.

An example of what I would say when I introduce myself to a real estate agent or a vendor:

"Good afternoon, sir! My name is Marc Mousseau. My business partner and I have been looking at the property that you have listed for sale with 'John Smith' realtor. My partner and I have looked at the limited financial statements that you supplied us and based on my partner's recommendation, we would be interested in . . ."

- ✓ getting more information
- ✓ making an offer
- ✓ the maximum we could offer for your property is...
- ✓ getting the vendor to look at the possibility of...
- ✓ we require the following to better evaluate...

Now could your partner be your real estate coach as well? Absolutely! Could it be your financial advisor or your lender? Yes, of course!

To help my students succeed in their negotiation process, I often act as their partner and will jump in when they are ready to make an offer to purchase, or when they are ready to negotiate with their real estate agents or the vendor. I ask them to connect me to their conversation on a three-way call and allow me to take on "the bad guy" role and act as their partner.

The best possible leverage that you can have while negotiating on a property is when one of you says, "I don't want to buy this property", and walks away.

#4 Limiting Beliefs

What is limiting you from achieving your goals? **Limiting beliefs are beliefs that prevent you from achieving your ultimate goals.**

Throughout my professional career I've stumbled upon many different limiting beliefs, here are some of the biggest and most common ones that new real estate investors have:

"I can't do this, it's too complicated!"

First of all, I want to point out that real estate is not rocket science. Realistically, there's no reason why anybody would not be able to do it. A 16-year-old kid can go out and buy a real estate property. My son bought his first house at the age of 20. And he owns two houses now. *So can anybody do it?* Absolutely!

"I'm not smart enough to do this."

Guess what, guys? Learn, read, and educate yourself! You don't have to learn all this in one day. Even if it takes you a year to understand what you're doing, for example how to write a good offer of purchase - so what? Remember, **Rome was not built in a day!**

"I don't have the kind of money to do real estate."

You have to understand that you don't need money to get into this business. What you really need is knowledge and the ability to find a good deal. If you find a good deal, you will find the money. It's that simple!

I may offend some people, but some ladies are saying:

"I'm not going to succeed, because I'm a woman."

Well, that is totally false! Women are as capable as men in real estate and there are many good examples of very successful women out there. This is not a reason to limit yourself or avoid real estate. Anyone could do it!

"I want to go and see the properties before I buy, or before I make an offer of purchase."

This is totally wrong! In reality, you actually *don't* want to go see a property before you make an offer of purchase. You make your offer based on numbers, not on what the property looks like. Then you re-negotiate based on what the property looks like, or on your inspector's report.

I often hear people claiming:

"There are no deals out there."

Not true at all! **There are deals everywhere!**

Some real estate investors say:

"*I don't know where to start looking.*"

Maybe you should start buying close to where you live, on your turf.

There will always be:
- People getting divorced;
- People losing their jobs;
- People that cannot afford the negative cash flow anymore;
- People that might have health challenges;
- Fights over partnerships.

All those reasons could force people to sell their property. You just need to find that motivated vendor and follow your plan and strategy.

#5 Self-discipline

How disciplined are you? What do you need to do to make sure that you thrive?

There are only 24 hours in a day and only 7 days in a week. We all know that, but how you use your time and how disciplined you are about using that valuable time is what counts here!

We have to start planning our time - our days, our weeks, our month!

One of the first things I emphasize in front of my students is that you should plan on spending a minimum of 10 hours a week as a part-time real estate entrepreneur.

What I recommend is the following:
- **Tuesday night** - three hours working
- **Thursday night** - three hours working
- **Saturday morning** - four hours working

The reason I specify Tuesday and Thursday as working days is because on Tuesday you can call people and gather information, on Thursday you run numbers and on Saturday you contact vendors, make offers and so on...

The idea behind this planning is very, very simple - if you don't schedule it, it will not happen!

It is very easy to find a way not to do what we have to do in order to succeed. There are so many excuses out there, it is unbelievable: friends calling us for dinner; sport events with buddies, etc. Now let me ask you one simple question: if you were to invest, let's say $200,000-$300,000 in a franchise like Subway for example, *wouldn't you commit to being there?*

The first thing you need to do is **to fully commit to that schedule**. You are running a business! Schedule your time, schedule your calls, **schedule...schedule...schedule**!

Jean Lebeau, my business partner, is scheduling his time into 15 minutes increments everyday of the week. When I call him out of the blues, as a friend, me, his business partner, this is what he usually tells me:

"Marc, I'm busy. The next time I can talk to you is Tuesday, next week, at 1:30 pm. How much time do you need?"

...and he's my most successful student!

My point is that Jean has succeeded because one of his core strengths is that he is disciplined enough to schedule his time in increments of 15 minutes all day.

Scheduling your time will force you to have a plan and follow up on it! It will prevent you from "spinning your wheels", meaning you don't know what to do.

Here is a sample of what your schedule could be:
- **Tuesday night** - I have got to call 10 realtors, get four property information listings.
- **Thursday** - I'm going to run numbers and prepare offers.
- **Saturday** - offer time!

Don't waste your time, because one thing that you have to understand is that:

Time is not money! Time is way more important than money, because you can replace money, but you can never replace time. Stop wasting your time!

How much do you worth?

Let's say that you want to make $100,000 from real estate next year, we have 50 weeks. Your value per week is $100,000/50 = $2000 a week.

If you invest 10 hours a week, each hour of work that you do on real estate is worth $200, right?

If you are worth $200 an hour, this means that anything that's hindering you and is causing you to make less than $200 per hour, you should not do! Right? If so, then everything that you can have done for less than $200 an hour, you should sub-contract it.

Why would you paint a suite when you know that you can hire a painter for $40 an hour? Why would you clean the hallways when you can have a cleaning crew for $20 an hour? Why would you collect the rents or go the landlord and tenancy boards when you could pay a property manager 6% of the rental income? You are making more money in negotiating deals and buying real estate than doing these chores!

When evaluating your expenses on a property, always take into consideration that you will have work performed by other people. Calculate that you will hire a property manager, a landscaping guy, someone to clean the units when units are vacant, someone to paint, someone to do repairs, etc.

If you decide to do it yourself - good. But remember the golden rule: **if you can get someone to do the work for less than what you are worth, do it!**

#6 Go Big Or Go Home

What are you capable of? Why would you limit yourself to small stuff?

A lot of investors look at investing in real estate and they say, "We're going to start with the small stuff. We're going to start with a single-family home. We're going to start with a little duplex, and we're going to put all our efforts in that kind of property."

Think about it for a second! If you have a single-family home and the only tenant that you have leaves, you are 100% vacant. But if you have a fourplex and one of them leaves, you have only 25% vacancy.

You should also always bear in mind that it's easier to find financing on bigger stuff than it is on single-family homes.

Don't limit yourself to small stuff! Look at what your plan is and how could you implement it at best.

My recommendation is "go big or go home"! Why not *look at buying a six-plex instead?* On one hand, it might take you six months to find the right deal instead of three, but in reality it's the same amount of work, the same number of offers.

But on the other hand, the end result and the reward is five to ten times bigger. So, my advice is to look for bigger stuff, aim high, don't have fear, and get coached about it!

#7 Realtor

What type of real estate agents should I work with?

First of all, you have to understand that there are two types of real estate agents out there. The ones that specialize in selling single-family homes to owner-occupant and the ones that deal with real estate entrepreneurs.

You want to deal with the latter type of agents. They know and understand your needs. Those agents are capable of putting the deals in place. They also know the value of working with an entrepreneur that will buy 2, 5, or maybe 10 units over the next few years.

It's imperative that you find the proper real estate agent. Evaluate their knowledge base, interview them, ask them questions. Question them about how many years they've been in the business; how many real estate properties have they sold; do they do commercial real estate; have them explain to you what a CAP Rate is; have them explain to you what GRM is; why cash-on-cash return is important for an investor etc. Only then you can decide whether you will want to work with them or not.

You may also know friends of yours that are real estate agents. You have to ask yourself the question though, *in case they have not bought any real estate as an investor yet, how useful could they be?* This means that you may have to train them and this also means that you are paying $200 an hour to train someone.

There will come a point in time when you will actually know more about real estate than that particular real estate agent.

#8 Knowing Your Strengths

Do you know your strengths?

I would recommend that you make a list of your strengths. Whatever you're good at. Are you good at negotiations or at numbers, are you a "people" person, do you like to make calls, are you analytical, are you sales-oriented and so on. Simply, what are you good at? Ask yourself, "What is it that I like to do in real estate?"

Once you've made that list, concentrate on your skills and make sure to find a partner that could be complementing your strengths in order to make you more effective and successful.

Again, the perfect example was Jean and me. I was the guy putting the deals together, thinking outside the box, and Jean was the technical person, so our partnership thrived!

What about your weaknesses? Make a list of your weaknesses as well and ask yourself this question, "what you are going to do about it?"

#9 Patience

Real estate is not a **"get-rich-quick" scheme**. The reason I include the matter of patience here is because if you want to succeed in real estate, you have to be aware of the fact that it will take time. **It is absolutely crucial to be patient!** If you have a good plan in place and you follow it, the plan will work for you.

I have designed a plan called **"Freedom-15"** and If you were to follow my plan, you would be able to retire in 15 years with more money than you can spend, tax free. And the beauty of this is that plan renews itself every 15 years to perpetuity.

This means that if you follow my plan and if you are 20 years old at the moment, by the age of 35 you'll never have to work one more day in your life. How about that? ***Visit: www.freedom-15.com***

Another important question to ask yourself is: "Do you really, really need to have six units this year? Or could you be patient and wait to find the right property, maybe a nine-plex that has positive cashflow in 14 months?"

Always look at the big picture, what it will give you in five, ten, fifteen years from now and follow your plan!

Most importantly - **don't despair! Be patient!** Remember the 50–6–2–1 rule! Be realistic in what you're doing and also understand that starting your business is going to be more painful and difficult than after you gather more experience and know what you're doing.

It will take you longer to analyze the first three deals than it will take you for your 31st, or 57th, or 100th property, and that's absolutely understandable.

It might take you two and a half hours on your first one, but with time this process will get a lot easier for you.

Now it takes me two and a half minutes to analyze a property and tell you whether the deal is going to be good or not.

#10 Commitments

Make a strong commitment to follow your plan! **You have to be accountable!** Tell other people what your plan is! Tell them, write it down, put it on your website - "this is what I want to accomplish". Don't be afraid to announce it to the world!

Tell your brother: "Listen, I'm buying a six-plex this year. It's probably going to take me 12 months. But my first month I'm going to get this done, my second month I expect to do that, my third month I'm going to accomplish that and so on And by the end of the year, I will own a six-plex."

Don't hesitate to post your business plan on your webpage and follow it up!

So, what does it take to succeed? The matters I've addressed in this chapter are all key characteristics that are absolutely primal for your future success in real estate.

Chapter III
Do You Have a Plan?

Having a plan is key to achieving your goals. *But how can you put a good plan together?*

Actually, it's quite simple. In order to plan something you need to know what you want to accomplish at the end.

It's plain and simple - **plan with the end in sight**! Let's say for example that you want to own 500 units in five years.

- ✓ That is 100 units per year, do we agree? True!
- ✓ Do you agree that it's 50 units per 6 months? Yes!
- ✓ And that is 25 units per 3 months.
- ✓ And 8 units per month.
- ✓ It means only 2 units per week.

We get these numbers just by putting the end goal in perspective and cutting it down based on the time period.

The difficult part is to get this process started. It will take you longer to buy your first six-plex now, compared to how long it will take you to buy the same type of building in two years from now,

The same could be true for buying a 45-unit building today. It might take you a year and a half to find one and to buy one, but once you acquire a few buildings and have the necessary experience, it won't take you as long.

So, let's start with the end result in mind!

Same example - 500 units for 5 years. We know that the further ahead in time we go, the easier it will be for you to buy a 60-unit or a 90-unit building. It makes sense because:

- ✓ You will already be experienced on how to find good deals;
- ✓ You will know how to negotiate;
- ✓ You will know how to talk to vendors;
- ✓ You will know how to put in place "a no money down" deal;
- ✓ You will know how to attract partners;
- ✓ You will know how to structure your deals;
- ✓ You will know where to look;
- ✓ You will have new money;
- ✓ You will have a track record of success;
- ✓ You will have your website;

- ✓ You will be branded;
- ✓ You will know how to make offers.

Now, understanding this, should you change and re-set your acquisition goals?

We still aim for 500 units, but we know that the biggest challenge is starting, so let's allow more time to acquire the first few units.

As time will pass it will become easier and easier to make deals and therefore you can accelerate your acquisitions plan in the future.

Be realistic, so that you don't get easily discouraged as time passes. As an example of this, let's say that it takes you 1 hour to do your financial analysis on your first property. *How long will it take you to do your 50th analysis?* Probably 5 minutes. *What about after the 100th analysis?* 1 minute. The same is true for negotiations, sales techniques, etc. It will be much easier for you to buy a six-plex in 18 months, than it is right now!

Acquisition goals per year:

- ✓ Year 5 - Goal 200 units
- ✓ Year 4 - Goal 125 units
- ✓ Year 3 - Goal 100 units
- ✓ Year 2 - Goal 50 units
- ✓ Year 1- Goal 25 units

Do you agree that this is more realistic than setting a goal of 100 units per year? You still obtain the same results, but realistically this is a lot more achievable!

Ask yourself: "If my goal is to buy 25 units in the first year, how long will it take me to buy those 25 units?"

Here is the challenge of going small - if you're buying single-family homes, imagine how many offers you're going to have to make and how long it will take you. But if you're looking at 6-, 8-, or 12-unit building, you can say:

"Let's split the year in two. I think that I'm going to be able to buy 15 units in my second half of the first year.

And I'll buy 10 units in my first six months.

This means, I need to buy 7 in my second trimester and I'll probably be able to buy 3 units in my first three months."

- ✓ 0-3 months - 3 units
- ✓ 3-6 months - 7 units
- ✓ 6-12 months -15 units

If I wanted to buy or acquire 25 units in one year, this is how I would plan my first year.

Even if you weren't able to buy exactly 25 units in your first year and you only bought 18, it would still be a success, because you followed the plan. You would just need to re-adjust your aim and move on!

How Many Offers Do You Need In Order To Achieve Your Goal?

If you remember the success ratio of 50–6–2–1, you know that if you want to acquire one property in the next 3 months you will have to put 50 offers out in order to buy 1 property.

Next you need to break down your work schedule even more! I recommend a commitment of 2 nights a week, Tuesday and Thursday evenings from 7:00pm to 10:00pm and Saturday morning 8:00am to 12:00am. That is 10 Hours a week.

Now let's plan on buying the first 3 units over the next three months.

How many offers of purchase do you need to make? If you're buying a triplex or a fourplex, this means that in the next three months you need to buy one property. *Do you agree?*

And if it's a fourplex, then you're ahead of the game, you've done your job.

So, you take the same approach - 12 weeks, 50 offers. How many offers would that be? It's 4 offers per week.

How many properties will you need to look at in order for you to make 4 offers per week? Between 10 to 15.

Every week you should look at 10 to 15 properties, you will probably need to contact 10 to 15 real estate agents to get information for you to be able to make that amount of offers.

If you need to contact 10 agents a week and it takes you 5 minutes per call, it will take approximately 1 hour.

Schedule it! "My first hour on Tuesday night from 7:00pm to 8:00pm, look at properties!"

Then from 8:00 to 9:00 call realtors to get information. Chances are they will call you back and you will play a bit of telephone tag, so plan on it!

From 9:00 to 10:00 gather information, open your file folders and get ready to analyze properties. Do your quick math, qualify the properties, look at other properties as well.

So Tuesday nights are information gathering nights!

On Thursday you could run all your numbers, do your research, prepare potential offers and return calls.

Now that we have booked Tuesday and Thursday nights, we have to allocate what will we do on Saturday morning.

As soon as the offers are ready, send them out early Saturday morning and then call the realtor and start the negotiation. You have to dedicate 4 hours to that!

What we have here is a 10 hour week dedicated to your real estate business. That is the amount of time you will need to commit to succeed!

Remember to keep the end goal in sight and the need to implement the plan and commit to it! Tell your partner your new schedule! Close the door! Do whatever it takes to succeed!

One of the things that you should also realize is that if you don't do it, you're the one losing here, nobody else. If you don't follow this plan, you won't get those 3 units, you won't get those 5 units, you won't get those 12 units. You won't be able to afford what you're looking for in life, because you're not committing to it and you're not disciplined enough to do it.

If you follow your plan, you ought to reward yourself! And it's simple. If after three months you did fill up your filing cabinet with 50 offers of purchase, even if you have not closed on anything yet, you should reward yourself and your family!

You should say to your family: "Hey I've made my 50 offers of purchase according to my plan, I know something will come out of this! I should have at least one good deal in place. Let's go celebrate and have a great dinner together! I've done what I had to do in order for us to succeed and I have planned the financial future we want."

On the flip side, what happens if you did not follow up on your plan? If so, at least have the courage to tell your loved ones and your friends that you've screwed up and you didn't do what you had committed to doing.

At the end of the year, if you sit down and look at your filing cabinet and see that it only has 12, 36, or 50 or 63 offers, then you'll know that you did not follow the plan.

This is where you should question yourself:
- ✓ Did I go out with my friends and have a beer?
- ✓ Did I go to the movies, etc.?
- ✓ Did I cut my grass?
- ✓ Did I do some repairs on my house?

If you answer "yes" to these questions, it is now time to review your commitments to yourself and your family.

Question yourself: "What prevented me from doing what I had committed to do? Why didn't I do my calls?"

Remember that you will not buy real estate if you don't if you don't invest time into looking at real estate deals.

Nothing will happen if you don't pick up the phone! Nothing will happen if you don't make offers! Nothing will happen if you don't do your due diligence! And if you don't do any of that, you won't be able to retire the way you planned.

Did you know that people will do more to avoid pain than to gain pleasure? So, the more pain you put yourself in for not following through, the more you're going to follow through on doing what you need to do in order to accomplish your goals.

Let's say your goals are:
- ✓ to take 12 or 15 weeks of vacation;
- ✓ to have a comfortable cushion of cash;
- ✓ to be able to quit your job;
- ✓ to have the freedom to do what you want and when you want it.

Pretend that you want this to happen 3 years from now! But then, you aren't following up on your plan. *Guess what?* You're not going on vacation, no cash, same job, still chained to life...

So, follow your plan! Create pain! Remember that if there is enough pain, you will follow up!

As you know, I've been teaching for about 15 years now and I have been frequently asked by many students, what my plan was. Instead of giving you my plan, I decided to create one specifically for you.

The plan is called *"Freedom 15"*. And *"Freedom 15"* is very, very simple!

I wrote a book on it. You can visit my website **www.freedom-15.com**. It incorporates a software program that helps you visualize the power of this plan.

Again, the website's address is **www.freedom-15.com**. Go there right now and start planning your better future!

Chapter IV

What Kind of Property Should You Buy?

First let's establish the kind of properties that are out there in order for us to be able to prepare an investment plan. Basically there are five types of properties that you could buy and two specialized:

1. Single-family homes;
2. Small multi - 2 to 4 units;
3. Multi-unit walk-ups;
4. Multi high-rise;
5. Multi high-rise with amenities;
6. Commercial real estate;
7. Land

Single Family Homes

When looking at buying your first investment property or even your first property, what you should look for is a single-family home with a basement suite, or a duplex side-by-side, or one on top.

Why is that? By having a rental income from your basement suite you will lower your occupancy cost, while still enjoying ownership rights to the property.

As an example, a few years ago my son, age 21, bought his first property - a duplex with a basement suite. He rents his basement suite for $800 a month. His monthly payments (mortgage, insurance and taxes) are less then $760 a month. That way he's making $40 a month, and lives in the top floor for basically free.

Now if he wanted, he could rent the top floor for $1000 a month and be positive by $1040 a month. Unfortunately he needs to live somewhere.

Step #2 - now he is 24, he bought his second property. He is getting $750 for the basement and $1100 for the first floor, total $1850 a month in income. His expenses (mortgage, insurance and taxes) are still around $900 a month.

He is making $40 on his first property and $950 on his second house, for a total of almost $1000 a month. And on top of that he is living in one of his own houses, *what more do you want?!* So, single-family houses with basement suites are a great investment as a start up house. They are also great for cash flow, if you don't pay too much!

Though, the challenge as an investor with buying single-family houses is financing.

For a single-family home and a small multi (less then 4 units), financing is more complicated and difficult to obtain than anything else.

Why is that? When a bank or a financial institution looks at financing these types of units, they look at you, the borrower/investor, as the source of income to repay the debt.

Rarely will they calculate the rental income to help you pay for the principal, interest, and taxes "P.I.T.". If they did, most of the time they would only use 50% of the rental income.

What they do is add 50% of the rental income to your personal income and then take 100% of the expenses against your income. You can see that very quickly, you will be running out of disposable income to buy anything, as your debt ratio will be completely out of whack!

The other challenges banks have with "small stuff" are the effects that vacancies have on your cash flow.

Institutions are asking themselves the following question: "What if we have to foreclose on the property (the single-family home) and there is 1 unit vacant. We would have 100% vacancy. There's no income on it, so the risk is bigger."

These banking guidelines are sort of the norm and apply most of the time for small properties that are in the range from 1 to 4 units.

Multi-Units and Multi-Unit Walk-ups

Multi-unit are 4–5 or 6-unit buildings. Multi-unit walk-ups are multi level walk-up (4–4–4) buildings, 12-unit 6–6–6 building, or 18-units.

Usually in these types of buildings there is no elevator. By the way, these are the easiest units to buy and the easiest to finance respectively.

These types of units are considered commercial real estate, therefore you have to go to a commercial lender or a commercial loan officer to get loans.

On commercial investment properties financial institutions evaluate the value of the building and the loan that they would advance on the property, based on the income that the property generates. If the property can sustain a mortgage of "X", that is what the amount they will lend to you.

In other words, the financial institutions are willing to lend on the building's capabilities to carry the property by itself.

Will this building be able to pay for itself? They will do their own mathematical calculation, they will allocate their vacancy numbers, repairs, maintenance, and property management. Then, if the **Net Operating Income (NOI)** is sufficient to cover their debt-to-income ratio, then they will lend.

Multi-unit walk-ups should by far be the number one choice that new investors should look at when getting into real estate, they are key to maintaining a growth path.

Multi High-Rise

Large multi-units are buildings that have elevators. Example: a 6-storey high-rise with 8 suites per floor, a 48-unit building.

In my opinion, this is the best of both worlds. Usually it has a concrete-based construction, it offers longevity, the shell or common area can easily be updated. It allows an easy condo conversion, it has potential for increases in rents etc. Multi High-Rises present a great chance of achieving excellent profit on re-sale value as well.

They normally are not a full service or amenities building with a pool, a sauna etc. **They have the least expense-to-income ratio.**

The great thing about these types of buildings is that you may not need a full time caretaker, full time maintenance team or HVAC people.

This is the kind of property you should aim for, as you progress into your career.

Multi High-Rise With Amenities

Then we get to **Multi High-Rise buildings**. High-rises are naturally 50, 100, 200 units or more. Normally they are full amenities service buildings - they have a pool, a sauna, a resident caretaker, underground parking and a resident maintenance person. You may also have a leasing agent working on site.

Commercial Real Estate

Commercial Real Estate is awesome - it is basically bought based on returns. The good thing about commercial real estate is that it has a totally different breed of lending criteria, very often purchased under "a highest and best use plan". It offers long-term tenants, medical center, dental practices. Small strip malls are a good representation of this type of investment as well.

The challenge with commercial real estate is when you lose an anchor tenant. An anchor tenant is usually a tenant that draws clients to the area. In some cases Starbucks would be better than the mom and pop coffee place. Replacing an anchor tenant may take time and in this case money!

With regular commercial tenants, the inoccupancy period may be longer than normal at times, just because of competing markets, demand, availability of space or specialized requirements, but when you have a commercial tenant they seem to stay longer and be better tenants.

You may be in for a vacancy period that is much longer. And when you find one, the cost of tenant improvements may be astronomical.

Land

Buying land is probably the last thing you want to get into, except when you have the opportunity to take an option and that you know that you can flip the option quickly!

Land investments are extremely difficult to finance, as you have no income to offset taxes and debt service.

Quick recap - these are the different kinds of real estate you may want to purchase. My recommendation for a start-up investor is to look for a small four-plex and above.

Single-family homes are really a start-up investment, but keep in mind that wealth cannot be built on these types of property.

Duplexes, triplexes or four-plexes are also challenging, mostly because of the hardship of getting financing.

Multi-unit walk-ups is where you should aim your efforts. This kind of buildings is financed based on the income that it generates.

Multi high-rises with or without elevators are properties everyone should focus on, as they are excellent long-term wealth creators.

Commercial real estate, shopping centers, strip malls and professional buildings are bought for cash earnings stability.

Land flipping is great but development is for the big boys.

DOWNLOAD GREAT BONUSES AT:

www.mmousseau.com/bookbonuses

Chapter V

Are You Branded?

Who Are You?

Over the last 30 years I have met a lot of people in the real estate business and I must say that it was a lot easier for someone to become a real estate investor or a real estate entrepreneur 30 years ago than it is now!

The reality back then was that there were very few of us out there. It was almost like an elite group of people, calling themselves 'Real Estate Investors'.

But in today's economy more and more people are interested in getting into real estate, as one of their main retirement strategies.

Unfortunately, in today's world it doesn't work that way anymore. If you want credibility and if you want to be a well-known business person, to be recognized as a real estate entrepreneur, **you have to be branded.**

Personal Branding

Personal branding is the practice of people marketing themselves and their careers as brands. On the one hand Personal Branding also involves creating an asset by defining an individual's body, clothing, physical appearance, digital and online presence.

On the other hand it defines areas of knowledge as well, in a way that leads to an uniquely distinguishable and ideally memorable impression.

Personal Branding essentially is the ongoing process of establishing a prescribed image or impression in the mind of others about an individual.

Personal branding can often involve the application of one's name to various products. For example, the celebrity real estate mogul Donald Trump uses his last name extensively on his buildings and on the products he endorses (e.g. Trump Steaks).

You have to know who you are, but more importantly, the people you are dealing with need to know who you are.

Who Are You?

Unfortunately when you start in the real estate business, you are nobody! Nobody knows you, you don't have a track record. You have very little experience and you have very limited knowledge.

So, we have to establish you as the person to go to, as a person that knows what he's talking about. **Your brand has to become you!**

My question to you and the question that you should ask yourself is: *"Who actually are you?"*

You also need to ask: *why should someone partner with you? Why should someone send you information? Why should a seller deal with you, Mr. Mousseau, Mr. Smith, Mrs. Thompson? Why should they take you seriously when you say that you want to buy their property? Why should they accept to carry a mortgage at a 3% interest rate - don't you have any money to invest? Why should they deal and consider your offer at all?*

The branding part of your business image is crucial in order for you to be able to get those deals, to get to be known, to get to be the "go to" person.

I am coaching one of my students, a former Olympian. He has no real estate experience at all and is just starting his investment career, so for now he is just a normal investor. *How could he stand out in the crowd?*

Who is he? Why should I invest with him? Why should I have confidence in him?

How should he brand himself? Why not brand him as an Olympian? For all of his life he has been a person that has made a commitment to excellence. He's willing to make sacrifices to succeed, he's making personal commitments and following through, and he's doing what others aren't willing to do to get to the finish line first. He's putting all the necessary hard work into it, never questions his coach, he follows his plan and he's committed to training and practice in order to become the best. He has made a long-term commitment to his sports career.

Would you like to deal with a committed person like that or just a new real estate investor? What do you think?

Check his web site: www.thefinishlineandbeyond.com

My point is that we have to find out who you are, what you're good at, what could you do better than others and of course, how to successfully market that.

One of the best ways to promote yourself in today's industry is to have your own website. People say to me: "What? I need to have a website now?" Well yes, you do, because in nowadays everybody checks everybody! Everybody goes online and checks who's "John Smith" etc.

It's not necessary to invest a fortune in an expensive website. You could have a basic website. Many web hosting companies are offering web building **WYSIWYG** (What You See Is What You Get) programs for free. Try it, spend some time on this, because preparing a website will force you to think about who, what, when and how you want to manage your business, and how you want to be viewed.

One of the free programs that I like to use is: www.wix.com

Your website should answer the following questions: who you are; where you are from; what is it that you are doing; what your goals are' what is your purpose; what is it that you want to accomplish; what are you looking for; what kind of properties are you interested in; what properties have you purchased so far; how much money have you made on what deal; what did you do to get there; how do they contact you; where do you want to buy and why etc.

On your website you should have a list of properties that you have purchased before. And if you haven't, then you should put information about a property that you're looking at right now. If you're looking at a six-plex, tell us, show us why you believe it is a good property. You should add some financial statements to it as well.

Who is your team? Some will say, "Marc, I don't have a team yet." Not true, you have a team! You have a coach, you have a mentor. You can go out and find a property management company in that area. Introduce them as your property managers on your website.

Add information about your accountant, your lawyer, your real estate agents, your inspector, your surveyor. They will all be happy to be a part of your team.

If they have anything to sell, have an affiliate link to their site as well.

Your website should also present information about what kind of properties you are looking for. If you have found a property that has a great cash flow post it on your site, explain why you think it is great!

It's absolutely crucial to add a "Contact" section on your website, a place where people could find out how to connect to you by phone, social media, or any other way.

Here are a few good service providers that I use regularly:
- Web Hosting: **Bluehost** (www.bluehost.com) is a great web provider.
- If you need some part-time work to be done by off-shore companies, **oDesk** (www.oDesk.com) is a good solution.
- If you need CRM and a contact management program, **Infusionsoft** (www.infusionsoft.com) is extremely good.
- **SurveyMonkey** (www.surveymonkey.com) is also great.
- Use www.Fiverr.com to get quick cheap designs
- 99Design.com for logos, websites, art, etc.; check them out, this is where I got my logos and brands made for less then $400.

I hear a lot of people complaining, "I can't afford this, I can't afford that." Guys, understand that you're going to need to spend money in order to be able to establish yourselves as professionals. It's as simple as that!

If you need a website to be built, you can have that done by offshore specialists (**Odesk**) for about $200-$300. The time it takes to find a good designer must also be taken into consideration when going this route.

Another challenge could be the language barrier, but if you are willing to forgo these challenges there is plenty of capable workers available out there for dirt cheap. Don't forget that a basic professional website built in Canada can cost you up to $2000-$3000. Some can go to thousands of dollars.

By the way, if you already do have a website, put a "squeeze" page on it. Offer a free report, lets say "10 free tips on how to buy a real estate in..."

You would be surprised at how many people will sign up to your site, just to get such a bonus and the free stuff you can offer them.

Once you have their name, enter them into your CRM program and follow up! Use a free CRM delivery program like **MailChimp** (www.mailchimp.com), or **ConstantContact** (www.constantcontact.com).

Following up will give you the opportunity to find new potential investors.

Phone Line

It's a good idea to have a separate phone line for your business. You should use "1-800" numbers, because they're affordable and will make you look professional in the eyes of your potential future business partners.

Have an independent line from the house, record a professional message. You absolutely don't want to have some message like: "Hey, you've reached the 'Thompson' family", or just "You've reached Tom or Jason".

Here is a quick script: "Hello, you've reached 'ABC' real estate", or "You've reached 'John Smith', real estate entrepreneur. Thank you for calling! If you need some information on the properties we have for rent, press 1. If you need information about..., press 2. If you need to contact me directly, please leave a message and it will be transferred directly to my extension."

There should not be any kids yapping, no dog barking, no noises in the background. Present yourself as a professional real estate investor who is on his way to becoming an entrepreneur!

Business Cards

Let's talk about business cards. Not to take anything away from one company or the other, but there are companies out there that offer extremely cheap-priced business cards.

Bear in mind that a cheap business card is nothing more than a cheap card, identifying you as being cheap! Often the paper is cheaper, the design looks cheaper and it does not look like a professional business card, period!

Remember that in life you always get what you pay for!

You have to get professionally designed business cards. Get a good logo, get a professionally printed, great looking business card.

By the way, remember that a business card has two sides, so make sure that you use both to your advantage.

Avoid colors like yellow, green, red and so on. You don't want to look like Mickey Mouse, you want to be a real estate entrepreneur!

Don't forget that when you go to a meeting, **your main goal is not to give out your business cards, but rather to be asked for your business card.** You want to get people interested in you enough to ask for your business card.

If they don't ask for your business card, it means that they're not really interested in anything that you've said.

You have to make yourself interesting to them. *How do we do that?* I'll discuss that matter and the "29-Second Business Pitch" in another chapter.

Often you end up home with 5, 10, 30 business cards and unfortunately you don't even remember who these people were.

Here's a quick and valuable tip for you how to easily remember who to follow-up with when you go to business meetings. I always separate the cards in two pockets - the ones that I have interest in connecting with in the future and the ones that I don't. I will simply put the card that I have no interest into my right pocket, where I keep my money.

The reason for that is very simple - money is something that I throw away, something that I spend, something that comes in and goes out. Therefore, that business card being in my right pocket is actually going to go out to the garbage.

My left hand pocket is usually empty at the start of a business event and if I put that business card in my left pocket, it is to be kept! *Why?* Because these cards are closest to my heart, therefore they are the business cards that I have to follow up with.

This is an easy way to differentiate who you want and who you don't want to call back later.

The matter of your personal presentation is vital to your success. **My advice - dress to impress!** You should always be overdressed, not underdressed. **Dress to impress!**

For those of you that are young and sporty - drop the baseball cap! I'm 55 years old and when I see someone wearing a baseball cap at a business meeting or wanting to partner with me, it just instantly turns me off.

Don't forget that you want to impress people with your appearance!

Are You a "yahoo"?

What do I mean by this question? Do you look like a "yahoo"? Do your business cards have an address at 123@yahoo.com, 123@gmail.com or 123@hotmail.com and so on?

Get your own domain name! When someone gives me a card with a 'Yahoo' address I basically question if they even have the money to buy real estate.

In today's world you must have your own domain name.

How To Talk To Millionaires?

When you attend meetings and one of your goals is to get to know people and create future partnerships, **don't talk about yourself!**

The easiest way to get somebody interested in you is to be interested in them. **Understand that people don't care about you, except if you care about them.**

Ask them about their business: how they got started; what were their biggest opportunities and challenges along the way; how long have they been in the business; what charity do they work with; do they have children; do they play sports etc.

If you are interested in them, people are going to get interested in you as well.

Believe me, people that only talk about themselves turn other people off!

I did a test exercise one day. I was in New York at a conference happy hour and I wanted to test my theory. *What would the outcome be if I just asked a question about the person that I was going to meet?*

So, I chose a good-looking woman and went for it. I introduced myself with very little information about me. Then I went on asking about her, what she was doing here, what was her purpose in coming to this event, what book was she writing, why did she write the book, where did she live, did she have any kids, where does she like to travel and so on.

After ½ hour I had not said one thing about myself, she had no clue about what I did, where I lived etc., she knew nothing at all. As we parted though, she said something that was very interesting. She said that I was one of the most interesting people she had ever met and spoken to! Yet, the truth is she knew nothing about me!

Here's another piece of advice - the best question you could ask someone that you want to build a relationship with is: **"What could I do to help you?"**

I believe that helping others is a key to my success. For instance, on one side of my business card I have the standard information: name, phone number, title, etc. On the other side you can see:

"Marc Mousseau"
"What can I help you with?"

This simple and honest question allows me to start a conversation with the person I am interested in and shows that I have a genuine interest in helping that particular person.

Remember that offering an unsolicited business card is only telling people that you are more interested in your well-being than theirs!

If you care about people genuinely and it comes out that way, then you will get the respect and the same attention respectively.

Then there is a great chance they will ask for your business card, because they are interested in you!

Chapter VI

Making Offers On Property
Buying Techniques

With over 15 years of training in real estate acquisition, I have seen many students and investors use different techniques to make offers on properties.

Some of them use what we call the **"shotgun"** approach, or the **"low ball"** approach.

In this chapter I will show you how to properly structure an offer in a way so that the vendor will be interested in pursuing your offer.

I'm going to outline my recommendations on how to do it and you'll recognize the right mindset that you must have, when you decide to make offers. Let's start by discussing the mistakes that real estate gurus won't ever tell you that you're making.

Shotgun Approach

Some real estate gurus advise their students to use the **"shotgun"** approach. Actually this is a very simple technique. You find properties that are for sale and prepare offers on all of them. You make ridiculously low offers and then you sit and wait to see what sticks.

Low Ball Approach

The other approach would be the **"low ball"** strategy. You just look at a property and if they are asking $660,000, you make an offer as low as $400,000 and see if you get a bite.

These types of approaches are very similar, except the fact that with the "shotgun" approach you blast out 150 offers in a very short period of time, hoping that one will stick.

With the "low ball" approach you take it one at a time, just one property. You "low ball" it and see what happens. The disadvantage of using this technique is that you very quickly burn your real estate agent's 'market'. If you're calling a real estate agent requesting information and you ask him to make a "low ball" offer on every one of the properties that he sends you, guess what? You won't have real estate agent friends for long. That real estate agent will definitely not have you as one of his great customers and he's going to think that you are wasting his time, and he would be right!

The "shotgun" and the "low ball" approach are strategies that will probably put you in a position where neither agents nor vendors will ever want to do business with you in the future.

Pre-Framing

Throughout my career in real estate, I have used a particular sales technique that I have personally named "**Pre-Framing**".

Even before you start negotiations, even before the real estate agent contacts the vendor and before he sends you some information on the property, **you want to pre-frame what will be happening**, who you are and what you're looking for, so that the real estate agent knows who is he going to be dealing with.

Naturally, the best way to do this is to say: "My name is Marc Mousseau. I am a real estate entrepreneur. My partner and I are looking at properties in this area of town. As real estate entrepreneur, we buy based on profitability, cash-on-cash return and on fair market value. If we are going to buy someone else's problem, we definitely want to make a profit on these properties. Please understand that we are looking for a deal, we are not interested in just buying someone else's problem."

By approaching the discussion in that manner, the real estate agent knows that you're not just some random guy who has attended a three-day seminar and decided to get into real estate.

You're pre-framing the fact that you have got a partner, that you're buying based on cash flow, that you're buying based on extensive research - on CAP rates, on GRM, on cost per door, on "1% rule", future fair market value, etc.

As an example of pre-framing - a few years ago I was with a vendor, actually on the roof of his high-rise building. This particular property was in a need of a lot of renovation. When I say "a lot of renovation" I mean hundreds of thousands of dollars worth of renovation.

The vendor wanted full retail price, as if this building was in a great shape. The property was in Hamilton, Ontario and I lived in Ottawa, Ontario at that time. In our discussion the vendor kept on saying that this work could be done very cheaply, because he knew so and so, that could get the work done at really, really low prices!

In the pre-framing of my offer, I had discussed with the vendor the fact that he was local and that he knew a lot of tradespeople. The challenge was that I was from out of town and the local companies would actually charge me a premium, just because of my lack of local knowledge and contacts.

In that way I took advantage of the fact that I'm pre-framing the arguments, which allowed me to justify my lower offer.

Another option for me could have been to actually be more precise with the vendor as to his estimate of the cost, to include all repair cost into the price and then to have the vendor perform the work before closing.

The Dating Principle Approach

This is my preferred technique in the art of making offers and negotiations.

The visual side of **"the dating principle" approach** is basically discussing or negotiating with the vendor, just like if we were dating.

If I'm a man who wants to date a woman and it just happens so that I insult the woman to start with, guess what? There will not be any dating!

I want to build a relationship with the vendor and I definitely want the vendor to like me. I would rather have the vendor say: "This gentleman, Marc, made me an offer. We don't really agree on price, but I like him. Therefore, I'd like to continue negotiations with him and find a way to put a deal together."

By using the dating principle strategy, it gives you a real chance to bring all the parties together (the vendor, the real estate agent and yourself) and it shows your firm intent to make that transaction.

As an example - a vendor would wants $1,000,000 for his property. You analyze the property and based on your numbers, CAP rate, GRM, "1% rule", whatever evaluation techniques that you're using, the property is worth on paper $810,000.

This is almost 20% off of the original price. If you turn around and offer the vendor $800,000 upfront, the chances are very, very, slim that you'll get further than just the presentation of your offer.

The real estate agent is going to kick back and say: "I can't accept this!" Some of them will even say that they will not present such a ridiculous offer to the vendor.

The vendor will definitely refuse it. The real estate agent may actually tell the vendor to refuse that kind of offer.

By making your first offer, your goal is to test the water and see what sort of threshold the vendor will accept. Will he accept carrying a mortgage; will he accept doing repairs; will he warrant the rents (guaranteeing a certain amount in rents); will he agree to do some of the repairs and maintenance; will he give you the opportunity to do due diligence and see if this property is really worth your price?

If the property has been listed at a million dollars, knowing that I don't really want to pay more than $800,000, knowing that I need to do my due diligence to confirm the valuation, I'd probably offer $906,735.

Now, some of you may be asking yourselves *why $906,735?* First of all, this is a number that I picked randomly. The real estate agent and the vendor receiving an offer that specific will also ask themselves that question: *"How did he come up with this price?"*

The right answer to that question is: "My partner and I, when we look at buying properties, we naturally look at certain ratios like CAP Rate, GRM, cash-on-cash return, return on investment, cost per door, profitability and 'highest and best use'. My partner, who is the technical guy, came up with this number and that is what we are offering. If you allow me to do my due diligence and you are able to show me that this property is worth more than this, then maybe we could come to an agreement. But at the moment, this is what my partner wants to offer on the property."

You have to understand my mindset here - if my offer were $800,000, there would have been no interest in it. The offer probably would have been refused without even receiving a counter offer.

But at $906,735 you might get a counter offer in the range of $935,000–$940,000. In that case you will know for sure that "the dating principle" has started.

You will move trough your due diligence and as you ask for more information, the vendor and the realtor will know that your partner is doing his numbers and that the price will not go up, but rather it might go down.

By the way, have you ever asked ask yourself, how did the vendor come up with a value of 1 million???

Negotiations

As we proceed with our offer of purchase and our negotiations, it's very important to understand that by having a partner involved in the process, you are just the carrier of the information. You're putting all the responsibility and all the negative aspects or demands on your partner.

For example you could say: "My partner did the numbers and based on his calculation, the maximum we could pay for this property is...", or "I wanted to offer you this amount ..., but my partner did not agree, Mr. Vendor. I thought that we could offer you 8%, but when my partner was doing the numbers on the second mortgage, he came back and said that the maximum we could pay is 4.25% in order for the cash flow to be good."

You could also say: "My partner actually has no interest in your building anymore. However, I'm interested in it, because it's closer to where I live. But my partner is the financial person here and he's the one bringing the money, therefore for him the purchase price is very important and you carrying the mortgage is very important. He is more interested in a cash-on-cash return than me. What I'm interested in is future appreciation!"

Using your partner in that way allows you to put the blame on him for everything that the vendor may not like or find acceptable.

Another clever way to use your partner to your advantage is to have him, and not you, simply "walk away" from the negotiations at the right moment. If you're on a conference call, you could almost pre-frame the fact that your partner is upset and basically rehearse the time when he will hang up on the vendor, leaving you with the responsibility of making amends.

This is exactly what we did on a Costa Rica project. My real business partner Jean Lebeau had rehearsed the fact that at one point he would say something specific and that would be the signal for me to blow a fuse, hang up and stop the negotiation.

The vendor would be insulted that I had hung up, the real estate agent would be saying to himself that he's just lost his sales commission. And then, my partner Jean would call the real estate agent back and say to him: "Look, Marc is really upset, but I know that I can calm him down, if you talk to your vendor. If you and I work together at putting this deal together, I am sure I could bring him back to the table.

So maybe there is a way we could save the deal. What do you think your vendor would be willing to give?"

This scenario works all the time when you have a strong and creative business partner. It's always an excellent weapon in your negotiations arsenal.

You have got to make sure that one of the partners involved is always willing to walk away and will always look like he's disinterested in the property.

Maximum Allowable Purchase Price Or "MAPP"

Another key point to bear in mind while you're negotiating or buying, is that you should always know and set what we call **"the Maximum Allowable Purchase Price" (MAPP)** of the property is ahead of time.

The MAPP should be the price where you're willing to walk away, where you'll decide whether to continue or not, where you tell the vendor: "We have to find a way to put this deal together, because we have reached my maximum allowable purchase price."

Once you reach your MAPP, walk away!

You never know, using your MAPP could also be a part of your purchasing strategy!

Using the Maximum Allowable Purchase Price technique is one great way to make an offer of purchase. You should start at a price that is less than your MAPP and be ready to go up a little bit at a time, but never more then your MAPP.

I have more pleasure in negotiating deals than the acquisition itself. You should enjoy this process, because the better you will get at negotiating deal, the more profitable your deals will be.

When negotiating deals, always ask yourself these two questions:
HOW CAN I MAKE THIS DEAL HAPPEN?
HOW CAN I MAKE THIS DEAL A WIN-WIN FOR BOTH PARTIES?

As soon as you master these two aspects of the real estate negotiation process, you will undoubtedly become an excellent negotiator!

DOWNLOAD GREAT BONUSES AT:
www.mmousseau.com/bookbonuses

Chapter VII

Looking For A No Money Down Deal

It is every investor's dream to buy real estate with no money. Nowadays it seems to be the new investor's only pre-occupation. The new investors want the first property that they look at to be bought with no money.

This is actually their biggest challenge. They'll look at properties and say: "How could I buy this property with no money down?"

Unfortunately, often they're not paying attention to the most important aspect in this process, namely is this property really a good deal?

Let me tell you something - if you find a good deal, there will always be someone willing to finance it through a bank loan, a hard money lender, a joint venture, a partnership etc.

If you find a deal, you will most definitely find the money that will allow you to put the least amount of your cash into it.

Do No Money Down Deals Really Exist?

So, do no money down deals really exist in real estate business? Yes, they do! There are deals out there where you could structure the transaction in such a way that they become "no money down" deals.

Remember my initial statement - you will need to make 100 offers of purchase in order for you to find a good deal and be able to structure the purchase into "a no money down" transaction.

Will the first property be no money down? Probably not, because new investors do not have the experience and the knowledge to put that kind of transaction together.

New investors get attached to or fall in love with the first few properties that they look at and only concentrate on buying that particular property. This is a mistake you should avoid.

As a new investor you must be detached from the emotional side of the acquisition. You have to remind yourself that you do not care if you're not buying that particular real estate and the only way you're going to buy it is if the financial model makes sense.

And for you a good financial model may be that you put no money down onto that property.

Should You Only Look For No Money Down Deals?

The simple answer to this question is no! Your number one goal is to find a deal. If you find a deal, there will be someone out there willing to finance it with you.

It's simple - if you find a deal, it means that there is equity, right?

If you've created instant equity and/or there is a positive cash-flow, *could this be shared between you and your financial partner? Isn't there someone out there that would be an interested investor willing to partner with you?* Think about it!

As an example - if you find a property that is worth $1,000,000 and you end up having an agreement to purchase it for $800,000, you have bought a property with an equity of $200,000. *Do we agree? $200,000?* If you were to do your balance sheet with this acquisition, it would show: **Asset $1,000,000, Liability $800,000**, therefore your net worth would be $200,000 more the day that you bought the property.

If you've bought this property and its worth is $1,000,000, and you've paid $800,000, *is there a chance that it could cash flow, let's say $3,000 a month?*

Could you find a financial partner, a joint venture, a hard money lender that will lend up to $800,000 in exchange of part-ownership to this property?

Can you offer the investor a split in cash-flow? Can you offer him a shared ownership 50/50, if he puts up the cash to buy the property? **Absolutely!**

Ask yourself that question: If you have a lot of money, would you be willing to put some of it on a property that on the day it was purchased automatically gave you 50% ownership, 50% of the equity and potentially 50% of the cash flow?

So, the offer to a hard money lender ("HML") to partner with you or to a joint venture, could be: "I will give you $100,000 of equity (50% of $200,000) and 50% of the cash-flow, in exchange of lending me $XXX to buy the property." Not a bad deal! *What do you think?*

The other good thing about bringing a partner in is that in the eyes of the bank, you and your partner have put the money to buy, therefore there should not be a problem about where the funds come from!

The offer to your partner could be anything. It could be a combination of interest and equity, or whatever you decide and agree upon with your partner.

The interest rate could be between 2% to 10%. The cash flow split could be between 30% to 100% and the ownership could be anything that you are willing to offer. This is all part of the negotiation process with the equity partner.

It doesn't matter, because *how much of your own personal money have you really put into this deal? How much of your own personal finances have you put in? What are you really at risk for?*

If it ends up that you have not put any of your money into this deal and you still acquire 50% of the equity and 50% of the income, *wouldn't that be a great deal for you*?

Some people question me about "what would be fair in splitting with a partner, should I go 50/50, 60/40 70/30, 35/65?"

Let me answer this bluntly - **the cost of money is not as important as it's availability.** In other words, who cares how much of the pie you have to give out? Because without this financial partner, you most probably would not have been be able to purchase the property in the first place.

Remembering that the cost of the money is not as important as its availability is the key to your success while negotiating joint ventures, partnership agreements and dealing with financial partners.

Chapter VIII
How To Find a Deal

In the previous chapters I have discussed at length the key aspects of finding a good deal. Now, let's establish how and where we could find a deal, and what components are required in order for you to put that deal together. In chapter VI I have outlined **"the shotgun approach"**, **"the low ball approach"**, **"the dating principal approach"** and so on.

I believe that the most successful strategy of putting "a no money down deal" together with a vendor is "the dating principle". The following are the six vital components and criteria you should pay close attention to:

#1 - The Vendor Must Like You

The vendor must believe in your story and must be willing to participate in your growth. He/she has to be happy to help you succeed.

If you're asking the vendor to carry terms and conditions, the number one objective is "the vendor must like you".

#2 - Think Creatively Right From The Get-Go!

What do I mean by this statement? In what other ways could you buy this property by putting the least amount of your money into it?

You must think outside the box! You must not listen to other people telling you that you need to put 20% or 25% down. The question should always be "how can I put this deal through with the least amount of my money"!

#3 - Find a Motivated Vendor!

You must find someone that wants to sell the property for whatever reason, at or below market value, preferably below market value with terms and conditions.

Some students often ask: "Why would somebody sell a property below market value?"

In reality there are many reasons why this could happen:

- It could be a divorce situation;
- The vendor may be faced with financial challenges;
- The vendor may have no interest into the asset, meaning the vendor is not interested in owning the real estate anymore;
- The vendor may have no other things more important for him to focus on than selling that particular piece of real estate;
- It may be that the property is vacant or partially vacant at this time;
- It may be that the property is under duress;
- It may be the vendors heirs have no interest into the real estate and they just want cash;
- It may be that the vendor has no heirs to pass the asset over to and would rather bequest cash instead;
- It may be that he is just fed up of dealing with bad tenants;
- It may be that it is time for him to cash out;
- It may be that it's time for the vendor to move out of town, province or country;
- The vendor may have tax problems;
- He might be close to bankruptcy;
- He may have bills to pay that are costing him 20% interest;
- The first mortgage may be called on the property at renewal;

- The hard money lender may want to be paid as part of the agreement;
- There may be a balloon payment that he has to do on another property;
- The owner may not be able to renew the insurance policy of the property etc.

Whatever motivation the vendor may have of selling the property, you should find it out. And naturally, the only way to find that out is by directly asking him:
- Why are you selling?
- How can the vacancy be so high?
- Why have you not increased your rents for the past 2 months?
- What is your ultimate goal?
- Are you divesting of your real estate portfolio?
- Do you have other properties? In case you do, would there be a way for us to put a deal together on all of them?
- Would you be willing to partner on some of these units, letting me do all the work, while you receive partial reward on these properties?

Finding a motivated vendor and his motivation to sell the property is your key goal in this process!

#4 – Looking For Distressed Properties

Another important ingredient to success is looking at distressed properties on the market. By distressed properties I mean both physically (unattended for and in bad shape), or properties that have not been managed and maintained to normal standards.

You can see where the vendor runs out of cash regularly by the upkeeping of his property. Clear signs of such a case may be: the roof being in a bad shape; corridors; balconies; painting; hallways; interior suites; appliances and so on.

#5 – Is There Equity On This Property Or Not?

Another vital aspect for having success is getting a deal or not is to answer this question:

Is there equity on this property?

You cannot extract or get a VTB from a vendor on a property that is 100% financed, or close to 100% loan-to-value. You can't get it!

The only circumstance allowing this to happen is, if the vendor is very wealthy and his personal wealth enables him to help you purchase the property. So, there has to be some equity somewhere in order for you to make a deal with the vendor.

#6 - Do You Really Need This Property In Your Portfolio?

Even if you've found a deal and it ends up to be "a no money down deal", there will come a time in your investment career that you will need to answer one or a few of these questions:

- Do you really need this deal in your portfolio?
- Will this help you achieve your goals of acquiring a decent real estate portfolio?
- If you were to put this deal together, will it have a negative impact on your future acquisitions?
- Would it limit your future growth?
- Do you need to have this headache?
- Will you really benefit from it?

Another important question you should regularly ask yourself is: "Why buy if this is not a great deal for me?"

Don't forget that when you're buying someone else's property, you're actually buying somebody else's problem.

Think about it for a second! *Why would a vendor sell a property that cash-flows well? Why would a vendor sell a property that he has no problems with?* The only reason why he sells it is because he either needs the cash, or it's a problem property.

It's imperative to ask yourself that question: *Why would you take somebody else's problem without a compensation, without equity, without some kind of value added to you?* You absolutely don't need that headache! You must believe that the work that you are going to put into it is worth the equity that you'll achieve from buying that property!

Chapter IX
Key Priorities To Buying a Real Estate

There are basically 7 key criteria and priorities that you should focus on in order for you to be able to decide whether you're buying a particular piece of real estate or not.

Priority #1: *You Make Money When You Buy Real Estate*

This is the number one and most important criteria to look for. If a property is worth $1,000,000 and you're buying it for $1,000,000, you haven't made anything yet. All you have accomplished is the fact that you have just bought somebody else's problem. Your balance sheet has an asset of $1,000,000, hopefully 100% financed, $1,000,000 in liability, In result, at the end of that transaction your balance sheet has not gone up, nor has it come down.

As a real estate entrepreneur, what you're looking for is to increase your net worth the minute you buy a property! Therefore, to follow our example of the property that is worth $1,000,000, if you're buying it at $865,000, you've made $135,000 in equity on the day you've purchased the property. So you made money in the buy!

Priority #2: *You Will Profit When You Sell*

By you working on the property, increasing rental income, tenancy quality, making some renovations, cleaning up etc., the property should go up in value and when you sell it, you should make a substantial profit. **Disposition of the asset minus acquisition of the asset equals profit!**

Priority #3: *Does This Property Cash-Flow?*
Yes or No?

As I mentioned earlier, **why would you buy a property that does not cash-flow?!** I still believe that 99% of the real estate investors should buy positive cash flowing properties, period! I just don't understand Investments Clubs that are promoting buying real estate, even if it does not cash-flow. I just don't see the point in buying such properties.

There are probably only a few reasons why someone should agree to buy a property that currently at the moment of acquisition does not cash-flow, such as:

- They need a tax write off;
- They are considering this a loss, as if they were contributing to their RRSP or 401K;
- They believe that the appreciation would be so high that it is worth taking a loss for a short period of time;
- They see a highest and best use strategy for the acquisition;
- They expect that they could flip the property quickly;
- They have a lot of money to invest and they regard that deal as a stable placement of their money.

As an example - a doctor for instance may not mind losing money on a property, because it is tax-deductible for him. It may be his way to increase his retirement package by calculating growth on the property. He could also calculate that when he makes a mortgage payment on the property, he actually force saves this amount!

If I was to lose $500 a month on a property, $6000 a year, and if at the same time it went up in price by $30,000 net in a year, my return if I sell the property after one year would be five fold - 500%.

The challenge with that strategy is that you are still losing $500 a month.

You think you can afford to lose it? And what happens if the appreciation is not what you had expected it to be and if it actually does not go up?

What happens if you lose your job? What happens if you get divorced? What happens if... Do you see my point here?

Priority #4: *Cash-on-Cash Return*

This is also a key criterion. There will be a point in time when you may have to put cash on the property, your own cash. *If you are investing your own money on the property, what would your cash-on-cash (COC) return be?*

Example - if you put $50,000 down on a property and it generates $5,000 positive cash-flow per year, your cash-on-cash return is 10%. You're making $5,000 on a $50,000 investment, $5,000/$50,000 equals a 10% of cash-on-cash return.

Some of you might be thinking: *"10% cash-on-cash is a good return."*

Well, I might have to disappoint you here, **actually it's not a good return!** A real estate investor, a true entrepreneur would look at a cash-on-cash return in the range of 35% to 50%, meaning that you will get all of the money you've invested back within two or three years.

Priority #5: *Having Good Terms and Conditions*

Looking for good terms and conditions should also be a priority, but in the order of things, it would rank as number 5 on the list, because I would rather have:

1. Make money in the buy.
2. Profit when I sell.
3. Have positive cash flow.
4. Have a good cash-on-cash return.
5. Have good terms and conditions.

Priority #6: *State Of Repairs*

Should you be worried of the fact that the property may be in a bad state of repairs at the moment? **No, actually this is exactly what you should be looking for!**

A real estate entrepreneur seeks a property that is beaten down and that needs tender loving care, because this is where you have a real opportunity to make the most money!

Priority #7: *Is The Area Where I Am Purchasing The Property Appreciating?*

Will the property appreciate? Yes or No?

It would be a bonus! Even if it went up by 1% per year, if you made money in the buy and it cash flowed, *do you really care?*

More important than having appreciation is to make a profit the moment you buy the property, to have a good regular cash-flow, to get an excellent cash-on-cash return, to have good terms and conditions, to have a property that requires minor and inexpensive cosmetic repairs etc.

So in reality, **Appreciation** **should always be your last and least sought after buying priority.**

DOWNLOAD GREAT BONUSES AT:

www.mmousseau.com/bookbonuses

Chapter X

The Art Of Negotiations

Will My First Offer Be The Final One?

First of all, you need to be aware of what actually the different parties are seeking while offers to purchase are presented. **On one hand, the vendor wants the highest price. On the other hand, the purchaser wants the lowest price.** And the real estate agent's interest is to bring both parties to an agreeable price and terms somewhere in the middle.

We all know that if the asking price on a property is $1,000,000 and you're going to offer $860,000, the real estate agent's job is to bring both the vendor and the purchaser to a mid-point, acceptable to both parties.

Now, you as a real estate entrepreneur are looking for the lowest price possible. Your goal is to get the lowest price and not go up in price to meet the vendor. *How do you* negotiate this transaction so that instead of meeting the vendor halfway up, you actually lower your price as the offer moves on?

Let me explain the strategy that I use for making offers in real estate. I have discussed the **"dating principle"** in a previous chapter. It's crucial that the vendor likes you in order for you to be able to re-negotiate the deal with him/her.

Making an offer to purchase to a vendor where both parties agree to terms and conditions has a direct impact on the vendor's psychology. The moment a vendor has accepted an offer, his initial mindset changes. For him the property is already sold.

He knows that it is not a done deal until it closes, but his mindset changes dramatically. Technically he has a deal, **IF** nothing goes wrong.

His thought process is: "Finally, I've sold my property. I have a deal. It will close in so many days." Usually one of the first things that this vendor says or does is, "Let's celebrate, we've sold the property", although all conditions have not been removed yet.

Some vendors already spent the money; what I mean by that is that they've already made plans to invest, to divest, to repay or gift themselves things. They've already contemplated that they have one less mortgage payment, one less insurance policy to pay and one less trouble tenant.

Usually they've already said to themselves, "With that much money I'm going to repay my debts. With that money I'm going to buy myself a car. With that money my family and I will be able to go on a vacation. With that money I'm going to repay my credit cards." All based only on the fact that the real estate property has been sold. The day that the vendor has an accepted offer to purchase, for him the deal is done.

At that point in time the vendor wants to close on that, just because his commitments have already been made mentally. As an example: "Honey, we've just sold the property, we could go on our month vacation together, when it closes."

Now let's say that three weeks later there are challenges in the due diligence and there is a real chance that the deal may fall apart. How would he go back to his partner or to his wife and say, "Well, we don't have the deal anymore, therefore we're not going on a vacation." Think about it honestly, we all think that way when we sell something.

Working With Multiple Offers

First of all, I, as a real estate entrepreneur would never work in a position where my offer is being compared to another offer. I refuse to be manipulated by the vendor and/or the real estate agent in forcing me to offer my best price upfront.

I also refuse to compete against other uneducated investors that are willing to pay the full asking price or more on a property. But still, some uneducated investors are still making offers of purchase, just to say that they're acquiring a real estate. So, I totally refuse to be in a such competing environment, when it comes to price on the property.

What I would rather do is notify the real estate agent that should any of these offers to purchase fall through, I'll be willing to consider at that time to put an offer in.

But I will never make the mistake to present my offer at the same time as other investors do. You should not neglect that aspect of the negotiation process and always try to avoid having competing offers on a property with other investors!

Being Prepared Is Key To Successful Negotiations

You decided to move ahead in a competing offer to purchase - **multiple offers scenario**. In that case a strategy that works is to put two offers at the same time. The first one is designed in such a way, just to compete.

In case the vendor's asking price on that particular property is let's say $1,000,000:
- ✓ Offer at $970,000;

- ✓ With the vendor carrying a mortgage in the amount of $170,000;
- ✓ With a subordination of a mortgage clause;
- ✓ With an assumption clause;
- ✓ With a substitution of collateral;
- ✓ With a first right of refusal clause;
- ✓ With a right to repay clause;
- ✓ Subject to due diligence;
- ✓ Subject to financing;
- ✓ Subject to inspection etc.

Or you could make a very clean offer:
- ✓ We know that "**Cash Is King**";
- ✓ We all know that "**Quick Closing Is King**";
- ✓ We know that the least amount of **"subject to"** in an offer to purchase is also **"king"**.

The offer would be something like this:
- ✓ Offer at $800,000;
- ✓ Cash;
- ✓ Closing in 30 days;
- ✓ Subject to due diligence.

By presenting two offers at the same time you put the vendor in a position that he has to accept either one of your offers, but because one of the offers has very little **"subject to"** and is **a cash deal**, there is a chance that he would prefer exactly that deal and decide to work with it.

Should I View The Property Before Making an Offer?

The short answer to that question is – no! **You actually do not want to see the property before making an offer; you don't need to see the property until you have an accepted offer.**

The reason for this is simple. What you need in order to make an offer to purchase is the basic financial information - the gross income and the expenses. Once you have that, you have to do your quick math to establish the real property value and then decide whether you want to make an offer on the property or not!

Prepare and present the offer, start the negotiation! See if both parties can get to an agreement on price, terms and conditions!

Once you have a deal in place, start your due diligence! The first thing to look at in due diligence is the income side of the business. The reasoning behind starting with the income first is that if the income is inaccurate or falsified, it puts the whole deal at jeopardy and keep in mind that this is your best opportunity and the most appropriate point in time to re-negotiate the deal, looking for even better terms or price.

Once you confirmed the income and that you are satisfied with it, then you proceed with the expenses - note that so far you have not spent anything! After the financial diligence is done, you call for your inspection. You want to be there for the inspection, this is where you visit the building and suites. This is the moment when once again strategy comes in.

If you see the property before the offer to purchase and you've visited the suites, you'd very well know the condition of the hallways, you'd very well aware of the condition of the building in general: flat roof, shingles, parking lot, landscaping and so on. You'll also know what the interior of the suites looks like: age of the appliances, the condition of the paint, the condition of the carpets, bathrooms etc.

How could you re-negotiate the deal if you've seen all this before putting a price on the property?

The best strategy I recommend to use is to put an offer to purchase based only on numbers and then you re-negotiate based on the viewing of the property and your personal inspection.

The script you could use would go something like this: "Mr. Vendor, when I presented you with the offer to purchase, it was based on (whatever condition) the property. Upon my visit I noticed that the roof needs to be repaired, there are windows that need to be changed, the carpets in the hallways need to be redone, the common area needs to be repainted and refreshed, the appliances in the suites are all yellow or avocado colors, there's mold in the bathrooms, the parking lot must be redone, etc. Therefore, in the offer that I've made you, I cannot in all due respect maintain that same price offer. That's why obviously we must re-negotiate this deal."

Also, as funny as this may seem, even the real estate agent involved in this transaction would be inclined to advise his client to accept the fact that the deal needs to be re-negotiated.

The agent has already made plans on how to spend his or her sales commission.

So, now you have both the vendor and the real estate agent wanting not to lose this deal and working together in order for all the parties to come to terms with this particular offer to purchase.

In conclusion to this chapter, I'd like to emphasize on the fact that when a vendor accepts an offer, in his mind he has already sold the property. **Expect to re-negotiate your deals as you do your due diligence.**

My advice is: never put yourself in a multiple offer situation, you will definitely pay too much and lose money!

Chapter XI

Do You Have Any Money?

The hard reality of not having money is always there for most of the new real estate investors. For some of you that already have 3 or 4 properties in your portfolio, you know that at some point in time you'll definitely run out of money.

And those of you that have multiple properties, luckily for you, you know the drill, namely how to find money in order for you to purchase more real estate. One thing that is certain is that we will always run out of money. The big question is **WHEN**!

My apologies, if I offend some people here, but as a brand new investor, unfortunately we have little to offer. *What can you offer an investor for him to be willing to become a partner of yours?*

Why would an investor partner with someone that's brand new to the real estate industry, that has little knowledge, that has no funds, **other than the fact that they** see in that person, potential, honesty, hard working, dedication and commitment, a person who's eager to learn?

Fortunately, when an investor, future partner or a potential joint venture partner sees that kind of skills and determination in you, there's a potential for partnerships.

I have discussed the matter of branding in chapter V. To be branded is an extremely important aspect in today's world. You have to show that you're serious about your business, about what you're doing, and your website is an absolutely vital ingredient in that process.

You have to think about your business image, who are you; why would someone lend you money! **One of the key points that you have to remember is that you must always portray the person that they want to invest in.**

Should You Train Your Real Estate Agent?

Very often when looking for properties, we deal with real estate agents as the first contact. These agents will forward to you information on the property that they have, based solely on their "gut feeling", on the impression left by your presentation, on your initial speech, on your demeanor, on your chances in being real in getting involved into that transaction.

When calling realtors use a script that sounds like this: "Mr. Real Estate Agent, my name is Marc Mousseau. My partner and I are looking at properties in your area. We've stumbled on your listing and we would like to get more information on it. Mr. Real Estate Agent, I promise not to waste your time, if you could please supply me with the necessary information for me to perform an initial assessment of the property using purchasing criteria and key indicators that my partner and I need. This would help us make an educated decision and potentially an offer to purchase."

When you are about to start calling real estate agents, memorize this or script a similar one that you feel comfortable with, as this will establish you as a straight forward, honest and up to the point business person.

Often the real estate agent will ask you a few questions in order to be able to qualify you. His first priority is to know whether you have the money that it takes to buy a property and how much experience you have.

Your answer to this question should be: "Mr. Real Estate Agent, my partner and I have the financial capabilities to buy millions of dollars in real estate, if the deal is good! When we have a good cash-on-cash return, equity upfront. If we manage to agree upon good terms and conditions with the vendor, we usually buy! But let me reinstate the fact that it has to be a good deal. We are real estate entrepreneurs and we are not going to buy property, except if the financial indicator gives us a "green light". I hope you understand what I mean by this, sir!"

In many cases, naturally we would like the vendor to participate in helping with financing.

You also want to know early in the conversation whether **the vendor is inclined and capable to carry a mortgage.** You also need to find out if the real estate agent understands what "a vendor take back mortgage is"! Ask the real estate agent if he thinks that the vendor would contemplate holding a mortgage. Ask him if he understands the advantages of a vendor carrying a mortgage (vendor take back mortgage; secondary financing).

If he does not understand what you're talking about and what your point is, which happens at times, it is your responsibility to explain to him these advantages and how to present to the vendor the fact that you do want to have the vendor involved in such a transaction.

While explaining to the real estate agent the reason why you want the vendor's participation in such a manner, you should also point out to the agent that the least amount of your cash that you put in, the more cash you'll have available in order to buy other properties, and you'd appreciate him helping you find these other properties and deals.

By saying it in this manner, the real estate agent realizes that this may not be one shot transaction, but you may be the client he's looking for, the one he'll sell multiple properties to within time. Therefore, there is an advantage to him understanding and selling to the vendor the terms and conditions that you may have included in your offer to purchase.

It is also a good practice to slip in into your discussion the cash-on-cash returns that you and your partner are looking for. **Again, blame your partner for being so stringent on these numbers.**

Example: "When looking at properties, my partner, the financial guy, is always looking at cash-on-cash return of approximately 35%. It's not me, I'd like to buy the real estate, but actually he's the numbers guy in this partnership."

This is a great way to defer responsibility to a third party that may or may not exist in reality.

How To Ask For Money?

As an entrepreneur, as a real estate business investor, you should always be on a lookout for partners. Anywhere you go with proper branding, with proper business cards, attitude, mindset and so on.

You should always let people know that you're a real estate entrepreneur and that you're looking at deals in whatever area, whatever town at that time. You should also let them know that you're actually working on a specific deal, information on that deal should be on your website, so that they could go to your site and see financial details of the property that you're looking at financing.

Always be on the lookout for financing and the easiest way to do this is to bluntly ask people: "Do you have any money to invest in real estate and/or do you know anyone that wants to invest with me on some of the properties that I'm looking at buying right now?"

Should You Go To Your Bank?

The answer is "No"! I truly believe that it's always a better option to deal with a **commercial mortgage broker**. A commercial mortgage broker is the one that specializes in putting commercial deals in place. This mortgage broker, is not the one that finds financing for a single-family home, but rather it is the broker who will put bigger deals in place.

Often they know commercial lenders, they know their requirements and they know their fees. But more importantly, there is a good chance that **the commercial mortgage broker knows hard money lenders as well**. They are usually the intermediary between the hard money lender and yourself, and they also have a personal relationship with these lenders. When looking for a good mortgage broker, key questions you should ask them are:
- Do they do commercial real estate?
- Do they have financing available in first mortgage?
- Do they have access to hard money lender?
- What are their fees to put the first mortgage in?
- What are their standard fees to put a hard money lender deal in?

- What is the average rate of interest the hard money lender lends at?
- Are there any upfront fees?
- Is it a 6-month or 12-month term? is there an option to renew and at what interest rate would that option be at?
- What kind of property are your hard money lenders willing to lend on?
- What would be the maximum your hard money lenders will be willing to lend on a loan-to-value ratio? In other words, would they be willing to lend 100% of 80% loan-to-value investment?

Where Will You Find Money?

For as long as I've been in the real estate business, I have very rarely seen new investors finding money while attending Networking groups, Investors meetings or Real Estate clubs. The reason for that is simple - most of the participants attending these events are actually people looking for money, not necessarily people having money to lend or looking for someone to lend it to. Therefore, you definitely have to rely on other ways in order to meet these people.

But whom should you ask? The answer to that question is, you have to look for professionals like lawyers, accountants, financial planners, doctors, construction contractors. Anybody who is interested but in reality does not have the time to do real estate, because they are earning good money.

This is where the question **"Do you have any money?"** or **"Do you know anyone that does?"** comes in handy.

Post on your website that you are looking for partners into a great deal that you are working on!

How Much Money Should You Pay Your Financial Partners?

Realistically, the cost of money is not as important as it's availability! My quick recommendation is that you pay a decent interest rate of 4%, 6%, or 8% and that you're willing to share a percentage of the profit if they put the money. You on the other hand found the deal, put the transaction in place did your homework, will manage it, and only when you will sell the property at a profit will you make real money.

Chapter XII

*Six Stumbling Blocks
That Will Prevent You From Succeeding
And 4 Tips That Will Get You Started!*

#1 Stumbling Block - *Who Do You Hang Around With?*

Based on my vast experience, I can't stress enough how important and influential the company of people you're in is. If you hang around with broke people, you will be broke! You are the average sum of the people you hang around with! Think about it - the people you normally spend your time with are very important to your future success, or lack thereof.

You will notice that technically you earn the average income of your average top five friends, the five people you frequently hang around with. You normally live in the same area, you act as they do, you spend as they do, you invest and waste your time as they do. Hence, the people you hang around with could be positive or detrimental to your chances of success.

You have to keep in mind, that most of the people around you will not understand your entrepreneurial vision. Some will most certainly not understand the fact that you're working so hard now, with so little results. They would not understand your long-term commitment to your future.

Unfortunately, by pursuing your dreams you may actually lose some of your friends, but that is the reality of life.

#2 Stumbling Block - *Watch Who You Take Advice From!*

How often have you asked your friends or neighbors the questions: "Should I buy this or should I buy that? What do you think of this, or what do you think of that?"

When you go to your neighbor and you ask him whether or not you should invest in real estate and he doesn't have any knowledge or experience in that business, *what kind of answer would you get from that person? What kind of recommendation would they give you and under what kind of knowledge are they basing their recommendation?*

If the person you're asking for advice has never been, or does not want to go towards where you're going and does not know what are you talking about, *how could he recommend moving forward or give you an advice on that particular topic?*

I have neighbors that spend their whole afternoon from 4 pm to 11 o'clock at night in their garage watching TV, having a drink with friends after their daily job is finished. *Should I go see that person and ask him if I should buy a real estate in Toronto, Detroit, or Florida?*

Should I do it, when this person's goals are not aligned with mine? Really, how much advice can I take from that person on my future? **Be very careful who you take advice from!**

You should consider advice from people that have been there, that have done it, that are doing it, that have the same vision, the same plan, the same values as you have, and from people that have sacrificed time and comfort in order to succeed in pursuing their ultimate career or life goals. In a nutshell - **never take advice from broke or incompetent people!**

#3 Stumbling Block - *Biggest Time-Wasters*

One of the biggest time-wasters there is right now is undoubtedly watching TV. Statistics is showing that the average person spends at least four to five hours per day in front of the TV.

Statistic Verification	
Source: BLS American Time Use Survey, A.C. Nielsen Co.	
Date Verified: 9.7.2013	

Total Use of Television	Data
Average time spent watching television (U.S.)	5:11 hours
White	5:02
Black	7:12
Hispanic	4:35
Asian	3:14
Years the average person will have spent watching TV	9 years

Why would you spend five hours of your day and 9 years of your life watching TV, when you can be spending two hours looking at properties and making offers of purchase for your future?

Why would you listen to commercials while you're watching TV, when there are machines out there, PVRs (Personal Video Recorder), that at least will allow you to skip commercials? Why wouldn't you want to use a program like Netflix, or just buy the movies that you want, instead of skimming TV for different popular shows for hours and hours?

Why would you watch the news, especially CNN or CBC, where every 30 minutes the same news is being presented? All those news media companies repeat almost the same news and what kind of news do you actually get from a news cast other than bad news, other than sensational news that everybody listens to?

It's okay listening to news once, but following news every half an hour on CBC, every half an hour on CNN, every half an hour on NBC, every half an hour on ABC, **listening four or five times to the same news is a total waste of time**.

You would be better off actually reading the national and local newspaper. Read national to get a feel of the economy.

The local news is necessary to be aware who is doing what in your area - is there a shopping mall extension; is there a new school being built; is there a hospital in planning; is there a Walmart coming to your area; what new advertising is there, that indicates a new potential for housing, new dentists, and all kind of services. In other words, the local news will inform you on what's happening in your area and could give you precious tips on where to look for your future investments and business growth.

#4 Stumbling Block – *People's Addiction To Computer Games*

Playing computer games is another big time-waster in today's world. People get addicted to playing computer games, which often hinders their chances of business success and having the life opportunities they dream of.

#5 Stumbling Block - *Attending Free Seminars*

One of the biggest time-wasters that I've ever seen is what we call in our business "the seminar junkies". Those of you who are reading this book, you may recognize yourself here.

I have heard countless times people telling me that they have attended every free seminar that was out there. They went to all these gurus in every different field that there is, all to get free information, but in reality they have never made the commitment to move forward.

Those who recognize themselves here - **you are wasting your time**! What you learn at free seminars is nothing more than quick tips on how to become wealthy, which are motivational to get you going, but if you're not taking any action, you are simply wasting your time.

After you leave the seminar, ask yourself the question: "What have I really learned and how could I apply it?" If you've learned something that was valuable, don't be afraid to invest your time trying to apply it and take advantage of it.

Don't keep saying to yourself, "I'm going to the next seminar and I'm going to learn." I am sorry to say it, but **this does not work**!

Very often I also see people taking notes in these events. They take a note on a hotel pad or on a loose-leaf binder. **If it's worth taking a note, it is worth keeping it!** You should have a business journal, where you can record all those thoughts, ideas and concepts that are valuable.

I've seen so many times people taking notes and throwing them away within a week, because technically it's just a piece of paper junk. So, buy yourself a hardbound paper journal, call it your business journal and in that journal record the good ideas that you've heard in these seminars.

One of the key things you must consider is that **there is nothing free in life!** Attending a free seminar is a teaser, it is a show piece of what the promoter has to offer you. And if you're not willing to pay to learn, then don't invest in real estate, because what will happen is that you're going to pay by the mistakes you are going to make later, just because you did not pay to learn it properly.

#6 Stumbling Block - *TV Shows Promoting House-Flipping*

Don't believe these popular TV shows that promote house-flipping. These shows are something you would definitely want to avoid as well. They promote how "easy" it is to do real estate, renovations and so on.

Let me ask you a question: *When you're looking at these shows, do you really believe that the people doing them are buying a property, closing let's say on a Friday and within one week this property is completely renovated from top to bottom, and it was done easily as the program shows?*

Don't you think that these companies, these promoters, these contractors, all these people already have a team in place, that they've already seen the plans, that they've already pre-ordered the material, that they've already designed their interior, that the contractors or the sub-contractors are waiting from the get-go to start doing their work?

Don't you think that the permits have been asked for in advance, that the pest control company is already notified that they'll have to come in?

These shows take about 2-3 months to prepare. *How could they do a show in half an hour or within a week?* Think about it! It just does not make sense that everybody is waiting to do the work that needs to be done on these properties, just because "John" has called his contractor.

There are teams in place for those TV shows, there is research in place, there are architects, designers and planners waiting for their turn. They already have contracts with trades that they've been using for years. These guys are only committed to making the show happen, therefore they are working 18 hours a day. **Just do not believe everything that you see on TV!** That's what it boils down to.

Tip #1:   Learn . . . Learn . . . Learn!

The last recommendation I have is - **LEARN . . . LEARN . . . LEARN!!!**

I'm a high school dropout and everything that I have learned I paid for. What I mean by this is, if I needed to learn marketing - I paid for a marketing class. If I needed to do sales - I paid for sales class.

Tip #2: Learn From Other People's Mistakes, Not Yours!

30 years ago there were no courses out there available for investors to learn how to buy a real estate, therefore what I know, I learned it by my own mistakes, or by having one of the best mentors there is, that coached me. So, learn what you need and don't ever be afraid or hesitate to invest in yourself!

Tip #3: Implementation Is Key To Success!

You must always keep in mind that it's not enough to only go to a class, you'll also need to implement what you have been taught. The key here is **learn—implement, learn—implement!!!**

Tip #4: Get Coached And Be Accountable!

Remember that it's in your best interest to be coached moving forward. *Why do I say this?* **Being coached by somebody who is experienced will keep you on track to your goals. Having a coach will make you accountable.**

Your coach will give you his/her insights into what you should do next. The coach will be there to help you and encourage you in moments of despair, and he/she will celebrate with you in the moments of success. The coach will be there to help you negotiate and put a deal together.

So my advice is - **GET COACHED!** The investment into coaching is an investment into your future!

DOWNLOAD GREAT BONUSES AT:

www.mmousseau.com/bookbonuses

Chapter XIII
Where Do I Go From Here?

Over the last few years I have had many students asking me, "Where do I start? What do I do next? Where should I look for properties?" My answer to these questions has always been the same: "Go to a store and buy a map of the area you live in. The next thing you need is a set of darts." People look at me and say, "What in the world is he talking about?"

It's simple! Put the map on the wall, take one dart and throw it at the map. Wherever your dart will land is where you're going to start looking for real estate deals.

The reason for this is very simple - there are deals everywhere and the market dictates the price of the properties. There are people out there that need to sell. *Who are they?* People that have lost their jobs, people that have health challenges, people that can't maintain their property anymore, people that are moving, people that are disillusioned about real estate etc.

You are looking for that one person, that motivated seller, who needs to sell. You have to understand that there's no need in saying: "Let's go to Detroit where I can buy properties between $1000-$5000." Because even if you buy properties at such low price, that is exactly what they are worth, nothing more.

Why not buy in your turf, where you might have to pay $300,000, but the market may dictate $350,000 to $400,000?

There's always a deal somewhere and your job, your goal is to find that particular deal. Remember that the price point is dictated by the market, by the global environment of where you're buying.

So where should you buy? In your backyard? Why not? That's great!

Now here is another challenge in buying in your backyard. The reality maybe that in your backyard price points are just not affordable and just don't make sense.

As an example, people living in Toronto, Vancouver or Los Angeles, or in any big city in North America for that matter, where prices are extremely high, what you'll notice is that you'll never have enough rental income to cover the high values of the properties. Therefore, if you are in that market it may be useful for you to look at other areas where you could buy an investment property that will cash flow. Unfortunately, it does not necessarily need to be in your backyard.

Look Where Other People Aren't

I have been to a few investment clubs where the investment club promotes itself as a guiding tool or gives recommendations as to where people should buy. I disagree with that practice.

Often the information that is used to lead people to buy is past economics - there's growth, there's a train coming in, there's a school being built etc. The investment club uses that information to give recommendations as to where you should go invest and that information is given to everybody. Now imagine, if the membership is 5,000 or 10,000 people and suddenly there is a flock of investors all heading to one city, to one area, wanting to buy a real estate just because someone else has said that it's time to buy there.

Think about what impact this flock of investors will have on property value. Naturally, it increases property value, it puts you in a competitive bidding war against a fellow real estate investor and hence you're not benefiting at all from following the pack.

You have to be ahead of the pack, not following it! Do your own research, listen to the news that is newsworthy, not the worthless media gossip.

You have to stop listening to everyone out there and start thinking where will there be growth in the future; where will there be a need for more housing; where will be the next university; where will be the next big factory; where will there be an employment boom; what requirements in the housing industry will arise based on a population growth; based on a new shopping center etc.? **Always think outside of the box!**

If I wanted to invest in housing, *where would I do it?*

Something to think about! Hurricane Sandy destroyed hundreds or even thousand of homes in New Jersey. *Would that be a place where you'd want to own a real estate right now or buy a property?*

I believe so! You might be surprised and ask why? *How many houses will need to be built, how many people will need to be lodged?*

Therefore, if you're buying right after the occurrence of a disaster, you will benefit from the economic boom in that area and you will be able to get good cash flow, while this is happening. Once the boom has settled down, you would be able to sell that particular property without any difficulties. Other people will buy it, because currently it has positive cash flow coming in.

You have to look to where your gut feeling is telling you the next economy boom is going to take place.

Warren Buffett's once said, "When I invest into a company, I invest into what I like out of that company. Is the coffee good? Is the service good? Are these guys going to grow?" He doesn't necessarily only look at the economic forecast.

Buying From Developers

A lot of people buy pre-construction in hopes that they will be able to re-sell the property when the developer has completed his project, they hope to get the best price.

The challenges with that kind of strategy is when you're buying from developers, the developer has already had 2 or 3 price increases, even before he launches the project. Have you noticed that when a developer launches a project he has great sales brochure, great show suites, a sales team is already in place, have you noticed that the minute the sales office opens there are already units sold.

There are two ways to make money from developers. One way of making a good deal is by buying pre-pre-pre-construction, when the developer only has a plan and the information is very limited as to what will be built, and at what prices.

Often developers pre-sell units just to create enough interest into the project. This enables them afterwards to obtain financing commitments from banks and financial institution. Often these purchasers are called "Founder's Group". This is the point in time when you can really have a good deal!

The other way to profit from such type of investment is by buying at the very end of the project, when there will be very few units left - the last 20 condos, the last 12 lots, the last 6 suites available. This is when you can negotiate a deal.

This is the right moment to negotiate to buy one property or the remainder of the properties, normally at a large discount. Most of the times, the only way the developer would agree to do this is if the developer protects his average sales price by giving you closing rebates, upgrades, furnished suites, rental guarantees etc.

As a creative financing module, you may also be able to negotiate a deal with the vendor, where if you buy 10 units at full price, the vendor will give you a tremendous saving on the 11th one. If he agrees to give you a 10% discount, technically you would get the 11th one for free.

Buying from a developer has to be done prior to the sales office being opened or at the end of the project and never on the day of the opening, because the sales hysteria jumps in, where everybody's just putting money upfront to reserve a suite in the project.

Quick Math

In order for anyone to quickly evaluate a property, you should use some quick rules of thumb. Some rules of thumb may be:

- GRM - "Gross Rent Multiplier";
- We might use the Cap Rate calculation;
- There is also one that is called "the 1% Rule";
- One that may be called "Cost Per Door";
- Another one may be the "Rule of 75";
- Your "Cash-on-Cash Return" (C.O.C.).

Averaging these indicators allows you to evaluate whether it's worth making an offer to purchase on the property or not. Knowing these indicators will also allow you to open discussions with the real estate agent and the vendor in order for you to find out whether such a deal is worth pursuing.

Quick Tip:

The quickest and simplest indicator of all is the **GRM**, **"the Gross Rent Multiplier"**.

GRM is very simple - it's seven (7), which means that if you have a property generating $50,000 of rental income per year and you multiply this by seven, it gives you a value of $350,000. This is the GRM value of the property!

Any time that you would pay more than seven times the gross rent, the property will not cash flow, if it's fully financed. And any time that you would pay less than $350,000 in this case, there's a good chance that the property will cash flow.

Any property will cash flow, depending on how much cash you put in. Example - you're buying a property for

$350,000 and you're putting $350,000 down. That property will definitely cash flow, but if you put no money down and you fully finance the property with different lenders, a bank, a hard money lender, a business partner or you use a personal line of credit or a credit card, all these sources of financing may have an effect on your combined average rate of interest borrowing.

Therefore, some properties will or will not cash flow based on that. **Remember that there is always money available for a good deal at a good rate!**

Chapter XIV
What Is Your Exit Strategy?

Many investors have questioned my reasoning in asking that question upfront, even before making an offer to purchase on a property. Whenever you look at a property, one of the first things you should ask yourself is: *What is my exit strategy? What am I going to do with this property?*

- Is this a short-term acquisition?
- Is this just a quick "**buy-fix-and-sell**"?
- Is this a "**buy and hold**", meaning that I will have it long-term?
- Is this a "**highest and best use**", which means what else can I do with this property in order to increase its value?
- Is this property to be purchased as an assignment, meaning that I will actually tie up the property and assign it to another investor?

These are the key questions you should ask yourself, even before you make an offer to purchase on the real estate, because the structure of your offer to purchase is all based on what are you going to do with the property in the future.

As an example - *what is most important in making an offer on a property that you want to assign?*

When I coach, I explain to my students that the most important factor to get in an assignment is not the price, but the longest removal of condition time possible.

On a "buy-fix-and sell" exit strategy, the key criteria are price and short-term terms. You need to have a good price, because you'll need to spend money on renovation. You'll also need to have some short-term financing, hopefully with the vendor. **Therefore, the price comes first, then short-term terms.**

On a **"buy and hold"** exit strategy, what do you need? Realistically, if you're going to hold the property, you need to know whether this property will cash flow, so in this case the numbers are important.

But what's more important than all that is having good terms. *Under what terms and conditions will you buy this property? Will the vendor participate with you in ownership? Will the vendor agree to give you some deal for the first few months, or the first few years?*

In exchange for terms, would you be willing to pay a little bit more for the property?

The fourth exit strategy that I want to address is **"highest and best use"**. With this strategy, the only thing that is important for you is terms, because you know that by doing certain actions, you will automatically increase the property value, so that you could sell it over a period of time. **Therefore, the price is not important, the terms of acquisition are.**

Your goal should always be to get the best price, but not to the detriment of terms, like for example vendor carrying financing.

In conclusion - you absolutely need to have an **Exit Strategy** in order for you to know how to properly write your offer to purchase.

Buyer Beware

In real estate like anything else, **things happen**. You may make an offer to purchase thinking that you're going to be assigning the contract, or you will be buying it, fixing it and selling it afterwards, or there may be "highest and best use" in the future for that property.

This is a WARNING - one of the most common mistakes made by real estate investors is that they don't ask themselves this very, very, very, very important question:

ARE YOU WILLING AND CAPABLE OF HOLDING THIS PROPERTY FOR AN EXTENDED PERIOD OF TIME, IF SOMETHING UNEXPECTED HAPPENS?

If you are not capable of holding this property, then you run into the risk that this property will:
- not be assignable;
- not sell using "Buy fix and sell" strategy;
- not be able to modify its usage "highest and best use";
- not cash flow "buy and hold".

Therefore, in reality you would be stuck with this property and that may actually challenge your financial well-being.

Chapter XV
The 29 Second Pitch

Who Are You?

Let me ask you a question - could you explain to me in less than 30 seconds who you are, what do you do, and what are you looking for?

This is what we call in our business **"the elevator pitch"**, or **"the 29 second pitch"**. This is what you need to say to anyone that you're meeting, that will ask you, "What do you do?"

In my example: "My name is Marc Mousseau. I'm a business strategist, and real estate catalyst. I have taught 35,000 students in North America and South Africa how to buy real estate and how to become more profitable in this business. I invest in real estate under only one criteria - it has to make money or else, I don't get into it." That is basically my quick, 29-second pitch.

You should prepare your own "elevator pitch". Write it, read it out loud - **it has to come naturally!** The questions you should ask yourself are: "Does what you say make sense? Is your pitch congruent to who you are, congruent to your brand, congruent to your knowledge?"

If you were a brand new investor, your pitch would be different. Example: "My name is John Smith. I am a new real estate investor. I'm looking for partners that would like to partner with me on properties that I have found, but always under the guidelines of my coach, my mentor and my trainer. Our goal is to buy properties that cash flow and that we automatically buy with equity."

You also have to make sure that this is really you. *Are you congruent with what you're saying about yourself? The image you project, is it really you?* You must make sure that basically your 29-second pitch is who you are and what you're looking for. So, master the art of the 29-second pitch!

Marc's official 29 second pitch:

*"My name is Marc Mousseau.
I am a business strategist and a real estate catalyst.
I have taught 35,000 students on three continents
on how to buy real estate
and how to successfully grow their business.
I invest in real estate
only when I make money in the purchase,
only if it cash flows,
only if I get a great cash on cash return.
I'm always open to new partnerships.
If you are interested, please let me know!
Now, tell me how I can help you
in your business?"*

DOWNLOAD GREAT BONUSES AT:

www.mmousseau.com/bookbonuses

Conclusion

My friends, my fellow real estate entrepreneurs, this journey has just begun. I want to thank you all for taking the time to read through this book. I am certain that you see that I am not a professional writer - I am more of a professional real estate entrepreneur, investor, trainer and coach.

As I have mentioned earlier, I'm a high school dropout, but at the same time I am a person that believes in himself and in others, and a person that has faith in the power of knowledge.

I sincerely wish all of you the best! I hope that you will use the guiding principles that I have written down for you in this book to your advantage. My strong belief is that anyone could do real estate and become successful in this business.

I thank you for having the time and motivation to read this book. I wish all of you the best of health, continued education, continued growth and success!

Live With Ultimate Passion!
Marc Mousseau

Bonuses

It has always been my belief that we should all **under-promise and over-deliver**. I have five bonuses that I almost kept secret, but decided to share. Believe me, no one could put a price tag on the value of the bonuses that I will offer to you right now.

Bonus #1: *Spreadsheets*

Some of them will save you time, some of them will help you and support you in order to properly evaluate your property in more detail. They will also allow you to evaluate financing, so that you can get to your net cash flow.

Bonus #2: *My Top 10 Clauses*

One of these bonuses is a MS Word document of my top 10 clauses that you may want to use in your offers to purchase. One of these clauses will allow you to pull away from any real estate transaction, for basically any reason you may deem appropriate.

Bonus #3: *The No Money Down Deal!*

Another bonus I want to offer you is a training program that I have recorded. I've included one of the chapters for your understanding and better comprehension of what 'no money down' deal requirements could be.

Bonus #4: *Top 10 Mistakes Real Estate Investors Do!*

This is a list of the top 10 real estate mistakes that new and seasoned investors have made. You will receive by email ten videos. Should you make those same mistake, you will have the opportunity to watch and understand the financial implications that they may have on achieving your success.

Bonus #5: *2-hour Coaching Call*

Listen to a recording of a coaching call with a student where I am coaching him on how to buy a 36-unit building!

I do hope that you enjoy this book and I hope that you'll be enjoying these top bonuses and videos.

Books From The Author

As you could see from the experience of the author, Marc has real estate knowledge beyond writing or creating just one book. He has written and is presently working on revisions of **"What Real Estate Gurus Don't Tell You, Or You Would Have To Pay a Fortune To Get"**. His second revision is scheduled for publishing for late February 2014.

As part of this series, you will have access to **"What Real Estate Gurus Don't Tell You"** about creative financing, property management, condo conversion, land development and understanding real estate financial math. The aforementioned topics will be available in 2014. For the latest release, please check our website at:

- www.WhatRealEstateGurusDontTellYou.com

    www.WREGDTY.com

Would you like to retire in 15 years with as much money that you can spend and have no tax to pay on that money. Marc wrote the book on it - **"Freedom-15"**. It explains this unique program and guides you step-by-step to its implementation. You can visit the website at:

- www.freedom_15.com

You want to buy with no money down? This program is a must. **"No Money Down Blueprint"** is another great 8-hour video program that Marc has recorded for you, plus the two hundred page manuscript that will guide you on how to buy real estate with no money:

- www.nomoneydownblueprint.com

Marc has also co-authored another great book called **"Dreammakers"**, with Jack Canfield, Bryan Tracy and nine of his fellow students and real estate entrepreneurs.

- www.thedreammakerstours.com

To contact Marc and order any of these books, please visit Marc's website at:

- www.mmousseau.com

Or send him an email at:

- marc@mmousseau.com

You can access Marc's products website at:

- www.WhatRealEstateGurusDontTellYou.com
- www.WREGDTY.com
- www.freedom-15.com
- www.nomoneydownblueprint.com
- www.thedreammakerstour.com

If you want to learn how you can write a book in only 10 weeks, visit my website where you will be able to follow how I wrote this book in 10 weeks. For more information go to:

- www.authorin10weeks.com

Made in the USA
Charleston, SC
02 March 2014